MW00618462

A NET of JEWELS

Other books by Ramesh S. Balsekar

Consciousness Speaks
The Final Truth
A Duet of One
From Consciousness to Consciousness
Experiencing The Teaching
Consciousness Writes
The Bhagavad Gita (commentary)
Explorations Into The Eternal
Experience of Immortality
Pointers From Nisargadatta Maharaj
Ripples (a booklet)

A NET of JEWELS

Ramesh S. Balsekar

edited by
Gary Starbuck

Advaita Press

Copyright © 1996 by

Ramesh S. Balsekar

First Published in United States Of America by

ADVAITA PRESS

P.O. Box 3479

Redondo Beach, California 90277

Designed by: Wayne Liquorman

Cover Art: Ted Kingdon

Printed by: McNaughton & Gunn

Library of Congress Catalog Card Number: 96-079929

ISBN 0-929448-15-4   0 9 8 7 6 5 4 3 2 1

Introduction

You hold in your hand a book of aphorisms culled from the numerous writings of the modern sage and teacher Ramesh S. Balsekar. The inherent problem with reading such a book can be compared to eating a huge box of assorted chocolates. If consumed in rapid succession, each delicious morsel quickly loses its individual character and dissolves into a sweet, amorphous mush. Satiated but compelled to continue eating, the hapless gorger finds himself ingesting handfuls of the wonderful tidbits with no appreciation whatsoever.

The solution, of course, is that rare and valuable commodity moderation. Taken one per sitting and savored with full attention, each piece reveals its depth, character and subtlety. Regretably, moderation is a trait not normally associated with seekers after Truth; therefore, we are presenting this collection of Ramesh's aphorisms in the form of individual daily morning and evening meditations.

It is important to remember that these meditations are not puzzles to be solved, coded messages to be "figured out" or vitamins to be swallowed whole, rather they are on the order of tasty treats to be held gently in one's intuitive heart and allowed to melt.

From such simple moments great Understanding is sometimes revealed.

Wayne Liquorman

Editor's Note To The Reader

This is a hit-and-run collection of the bare bones of Ramesh's teaching. For the flesh, go to his other more voluble written works. Better yet, go to Ramesh himself whose penetrating, humorous, loving and lovable presence cannot be put on paper.

Since Ramesh has asked me to contribute something here by way of personal history, I will say that from as early as I can remember my only consuming interest was to unravel the mystery of life to its uttermost finality. This impassioned predilection led over the years through a multifarious tapestry of experience and brought me into contact with various sages, some in person and some indirectly through their teachings. Among these, Ramana Maharshi and Nisargadatta Maharaj were the preeminent provocateurs, but both of them had already been snatched out of reach by death. In the case of Maharaj, reading his teachings was like putting on my own clothes for the first time. When he died before I could know him, I felt that there was no one left in the world to go to. But there was a lingering suspicion that no such torrent of voltage as had poured through him could possibly have just vanished, that it must have found an ongoing course through someone else. As to who that someone might be I had no clue until a few years later.

In 1987 I had just crossed the border into the U.S. from Mexico on my way to Colorado after eight months of prospecting for placer gold in remote regions of the Sierra Madre when a completely irrational impulse overtook me to go to California. Although I had no reason to go there, it became a virtual obsession until I finally gave in and turned west instead of north. A few days later found me looking at the Pacific Ocean in Santa Monica. Having been out of touch with the 20th century for most of the past year, the first thing I did was to go grazing in a nearby bookstore where the first book that came to hand was *Pointers From Nisargadatta Maharaj* [1] by Ramesh Balsekar. Noticing my interest, the proprietor asked me if I knew Ramesh. When I said no, but that I would like to, he informed me that Ramesh was at that very moment in Los Angeles on his first visit to the United States and that he was seeing small groups of people every day. The inexplicable compulsion that had sent me west from El Paso suddenly turned pregnant!

The next day, I walked into a room where about fifteen persons sat on the floor in rapt attention before a man who was speaking to them animatedly with a most unusual, soft intensity—Ramesh. Not more than a few minutes after I sat down, I knew. This was the man I had been waiting for, that inevitable singular link with Infinity who is the *guru*. I had come home. My road ended right then and there, at

---

1   Ramesh S. Balsekar, *Pointers From Nisargadatta Maharaj*, (Raleigh: Acorn Press, 1982)

the feet of Ramesh. That's what I knew then, and that's all I know now. Nothing else matters.

Whatever lies beyond where that road ended is as unspeakable as it has been unpredictable. Whether one's personal relationship with a man like Ramesh takes a demonstrative shape or a featureless one is immaterial because what is really going on is something altogether intangible. It sneaks up on you from behind when you're not looking. You can never put your finger on it, but it always has its finger on you. There are times when the ego unwittingly slips its guard and falls vulnerable to the least action of the *guru*, which can unleash unsuspected volcanic forces in tides and storms of love that exceed any human frame of reference.

What lurks behind the innocuous and seemingly ordinary person and behavior of the *guru* is of such surpassing subtlety that nothing can be said of it except that it tends to dissolve universes on contact. Relativity succumbs to a different order of magnitude. The *guru* is that person who is no person. He is every person. He is intimate and oceanic, a terminal enigma to the blindness of reason and its glaze of words. Space and time are afloat in him. He is literally All or Nothing. You know it when you know it. Then you are lost. No zone of private identity can long survive that double-edged effacement of the *guru's* love. In the company of one such as Ramesh there is no escape. You will be undeceived of yourself despite yourself. The danger is that you may die laughing.

Sooner or later we are engulfed by the fact that there is no more drama left in this puny play-pen of personal experience and that nothing in existence has ever been other than fully automatic right down to the last infinitesimal detail, like a revolving carousel on which everything that moves has been orchestrated by what is beyond it. And concealed in this ultimately unavoidable recognition is the secret of freedom, from which there is no turning back.

May you the reader be blessed with the grace of the *guru*, in that the brief hammer-blow utterances in this book suffice to drive the ineffable nail of TRUTH into your head once and for all.

Gary Starbuck
Santa Fe
New Mexico 1993

The universe is uncaused, like a net of jewels in which each is only the reflection of all the others in a fantastic interrelated harmony without end.

Self-Realization is effortless. What you are trying to find is what you *already are*.

Enlightenment is total emptiness of mind.
There is nothing you can do to get it. Any
effort you make can only be an obstruction to it.

If you but cease from useless conceptualizing, you will be what you are and what
you have always been.

At the phenomenal level the only thing
that is not a concept is this knowledge
which every single human being, every
single sentient being at every time in history, has known: I exist, I Am in this moment, here and now.

Seeing *truly* is not merely a change in the
direction of seeing but a change in its very
center, in which the seer himself disappears.

The only true understanding is that *nothing is, not even he who understands.*

Concepts can at best only serve to negate one another, as when one thorn is used to remove another. Once removed, both thorns must be thrown away. Only in deep silence do we leave concepts behind. Words and language deal only with concepts and so cannot approach Reality.

Between pure Awareness and Awareness reflected as consciousness there is a gap which the mind cannot cross. The reflection of the sun in a drop of dew is not the sun itself.

Manifestation may adopt any number of forms, but the substratum of all the myriad forms is Consciousness, without which there cannot be anything.

The source of Consciousness is Consciousness. Consciousness is all there is.

The universe goes on its merry, mystical, magical way until you start observing it and you, by observing it, create problems. The working of the universe has no problems.

We feel that we can exercise our volition, yet deep down we know that there is an order infinitely more powerful which seems to dictate our life.

The man of wisdom is devoid of ego even though he may *appear* to use it. His vacant or fasting mind is neither doing anything nor not doing anything. He is outside of volition, neither this nor that. He is everything and nothing.

There is no way you can control the consequences of your actions. Life is an impersonal flowing, and you cannot control
either your life or anybody else's life.

Real bliss is the absence of the wanting of
bliss. The enlightenment state is not wanting either bliss or anything else.

Enlightenment is merely an understanding in which there is no comprehender. It is a surrender in which there is no one to surrender anything.

Your doubts will never be totally destroyed until perception has gone beyond mere phenomenality, and such perception is not a matter of *will* but of *Grace*.

Only that which was prior to the appearance of this body-consciousness is your true identity. That is Reality. It is here and now, and there is no question of anyone being able to reach for it or grasp it.

When the sense of "me" disappears completely, duality vanishes in ecstasy.

To any conceptual problem there cannot be any valid answer except to see the problem in perspective as an empty thought. There is no such thing as a "problem" which is other than merely conceptual.

It is not possible to *make* the mind empty.

To meditate you don't have to have any objective, which means you don't have any expectation at all. In these moments you don't find Reality, the Reality finds you. Just sit quietly for a moment.

The entire phenomenal manifestation is based on the principle of duality, which starts with the sense "I AM".

Intellectual understanding is based on temporal cause and effect. Intuitive understanding is non-temporal, wherein cause and effect are one.

Without self-realization no virtue is genuine. It is only when you arrive at the deepest conviction that the same life flows through everything, and that you ARE that life, that you can begin to love naturally and spontaneously.

Man's dread of insecurity, and his hope of aid from a superior power against it, drive him to create the concept of a supernatural God. Yet this God and the very entity seeking security from it are *both* nothing but concepts.

As far as metaphysical duality is concerned, there is no conflict between opposites. Man's conflict between good and evil, pleasure and pain, happiness and unhappiness, is as unthinkable in nature as an electric current without both positive and negative polarity. The principle of polaric duality can only be understood metaphysically, through the willing *acceptance* of all interrelated opposites as the very basis of the universe and life therein.

True meditation means the annihilation of the ego. The ego doesn't want that. When meditation happens, promptly the mind says, "Stop wasting time; do something useful."

An experience is *never* factual but only conceptual. Whatever an experience may be, it is nonetheless only a happening in consciousness.

Silence of the mind which is the result of
a deep understanding, *that* meditation is
a natural, spontaneous meditation which
just happens.

When you *truly* realize that this life and
living is an absurdity, then you join in the
dance. You take part in this absurdity. The
body-mind organism continues to live in
the world, but without any sense of personal doership.

Problems need to be dissolved, not solved, because there is no solution. The only way the problems get dissolved is, as soon as they arise, they are merely witnessed.

When Truth is realized, there is neither bondage nor liberation. Both the worlds we dream of when asleep and this world we dream while awake will have disappeared into the cosmic dissolution, which is the equivalent of the state of deep sleep.

Love, as the word is generally understood, denotes separation, whereas in true non-objective relationship we do not *love* others, we ARE others.

Sensory experience cannot bind the person who treats it neither with zeal nor timidity but with *indifference*.

Absolute Presence is the ubiquitous eye that measures the universe. It is the center of infinity that sees everything and yet does not see because it is the seeing itself.

It is not the present which is fleeting past us with sickening speed. The present moment is indeed eternal. It is our imperfect perception that creates the horizontal succession in time. Sequential duration is a consequence of the single-track verbalization of our split-mind, which does not grasp the outer world instantaneously but interprets it perversely by extracting bits and pieces and calling them things and events.

The only condition for the realization of Truth is that the knowledge of it be desired with tremendous intensity. You cannot see IT, you cannot feel IT only because you do not really want IT - you are too preoccupied with enjoying and sorrowing over your finite existence.

The sense of being alive, being present, is so intoxicating that one is enchanted by the manifestation it presents and gets so involved as to forget to find out if the spectacle really exists or is merely a hallucination, a dream, a mirage.

Space and time, male and female, subject and object, being and nonbeing — all are lost in the flood of Realization.

Intellect is what brings about the sense of fear, because it is the intellect that rejects change and wants security.

For the human being which considers itself an entity to remain puzzled, Consciousness must produce new puzzles.
All that is happening is that Consciousness is amusing itself.

When the understanding arises that "This
too shall pass," whether it is happiness or
misery, that understanding will bring
about a tremendous change in perspective.

Only those who are able to see their own face without a mirror will be able to see their true nature. What kind of seeing is this? To see without the mirror is to see not with eyes seeing objects but as THAT which sees. It is the in-seeing or insight by Consciousness itself in which there is *no one who is seeing.*

When thought, discipline and experience have done their utmost and finally accept utter defeat, they then cease to function altogether. That state is beyond both words and silence. It is neither one thing nor another. The Absolute noumenon cannot be experienced. To know it is to BE it.

The knowledge of Truth comes about when dispassion arises in a man after he has learned from personal experience that whatever life provides is truly hollow. The man of the world becomes the man of wisdom through recognizing that non-attachment is liberation whereas the passion for sensory objects and experience is bondage.

Both bondage and the resulting suffering are based not merely on identification with the body but on identification with a wholly imaginary subjective entity *inferred from bodily identity.*

The very first thought "I AM" is the basis
of all further thought and indeed the very
source of the mind.

As water is serene when free of ripples, so
is the mind serene when free of thought,
when it is passive and fully receptive.
When quiet, the mind reflects Reality.
When absolutely motionless, it dissolves
and only Reality remains.

Trying to control the mind forcefully is like trying to flatten out waves with a board. It can only result in further disturbance.

The true understanding comes from outside. It is not of the space-time dimension. Therefore, we can only call it Grace. Keeping your being open and receptive to that other dimension is a matter of Grace.

You can't fight the ego. Accept the ego, and let it go on. This understanding will gradually push the ego back.

The result of man's intellectual development is that, unlike everything else in nature, he longs for a perfect or ideal harmony, which he has only conceptualized but has not actually experienced. This is the perpetual problem from which he will never free himself by means of effort.

The basic fallacy of man's search is that, instead of BEING the universal Consciousness or Absolute Principle which he noumenally IS, he endeavors to attain an imaginary ideal happiness in his existence as a phenomenal object by trying to become something else.

The dream world contains all the relevant features of the "actual" world. But the continued appearance of a thing is not proof of its reality, regardless of whether it appears to the dreaming mind or the waking senses. Only with the dissolution of all appearance does one awaken to the ultimate Reality of the Self.

When man accepts finally that he cannot make sense out of life on the basis of anything fixed, *then and only then can life make sense!*

The personal self or "me" imagines itself to be limited and confined to a particular body. Self-enquiry seeks the source of this spurious "me" by focusing on it the spotlight of attention or awareness, whereupon the "me" vanishes because it does not have any independent existence. It is revealed as being merely an illusion. What remains is that same universal Consciousness that was always already there as the true nature or very BEING of the artificial "me."

To be anxious is to wear oneself out. To seek power or to use force is to overstrain one's system.

If deep down inside you want most desperately to survive and be in control of things, you cannot genuinely take the attitude of not worrying about it. And trying to stop worry means making an effort to control. You must allow yourself the freedom to worry, to let the mind think whatever it wants to think.

The fact of the matter is: it is His Will which has always prevailed; it is His Will which is now prevailing; and it is His Will which will prevail in the future. That is a fact. The longer it takes one to accept that fact, the longer will one suffer.

Life and death are both concepts, the one being the absence of the other. The sage ignores such transient concepts and inheres in the noumenal presence which is everything. It is only matter that undergoes change or transformation and which is subject to birth or death, while the noumenal presence remains eternally changeless.

True surrender means in effect the acceptance of the fact that there is no individual entity with ability to act independently of God or the Self.

Contact with the awareness of the Absolute can come about only when the mind is fasting, when the process of conceptualization has utterly ceased. When the mind feasts, Reality disappears. When the mind fasts, *Reality enters.*

The non-action of the no-mind state is not generally apprehended in its true significance. On the contrary, it is misconstrued as idleness in a materialistic society where what is valued and expected is a furious competitive spirit to achieve particular goals. But what is forgotten is that all such thinking and action leads only to the achievement of a "success" that is soon found to be empty and ephemeral. One is finally left in ultimate frustration with the sense of having wasted one's life.

Organisms are created with certain given characteristics so that certain actions can take place.

All you can do is to act your role to the best of your ability. The consequences are not in your hands.

Change is the basis of life. Opposites are interconnected polarities, not irreconcilables over which we have to make a choice.

The original state of the noumenon is one where *we do not even know of our beingness.*

❖   ❖   ❖   ❖   ❖

Whenever there is the subjective experience of the "I" feeling, there is necessarily an absence of the "me" sense, of being separate, of being isolated, of being insecure. In the beginning a certain amount of patience is necessary to sit quietly without any specific purpose and let the "me" recede into the background along with the thought process based on it. But when it happens, the inner experience of unity with one's surroundings comes floating in, and you KNOW that *you are all that you see and all that you do not see.* The meaning of life then becomes utterly clear.

The question of how to live one's life is really misconceived. As an apparent entity man does not *live* his life but is BEING LIVED like a puppet on strings. All his attempts to "live his life" are nothing more than reactions to impulses engendered by psycho-physical conditions over which he has no control. All his supposed acts of volition are merely the fantasy of an artificial "me" notion which *believes* it is leading its own life of its own "free will".

The world is not illusory insofar as it is an expression of the unmanifest Absolute. What is indeed illusory is your mistaken identity as an independent entity.

Man considers himself a special, elect being apart from the rest of creation, but so far as the components of the physical construct are concerned there is *no* difference between various kinds of sentient creatures. Only the process differs. Your personality has come about only after birth and is clearly the result of a natural process in which neither you nor your parents had any choice. No individual has ever been consulted prior to birth about his issue from a particular set of parents, since prior to birth there was no personality to consult. Therefore, you have not even been party in any sense to the creation of the so-called independent individual you are supposed to be!

The effectiveness of words is clearly seen in the case of the manifested universe which is made by them to appear real although it is in fact an illusion. Then again, it is through words that the individual finally comes to realize his true nature when words and thought are ultimately sacrificed in the direct realization of the Absolute.

Anything that happens in the present moment is necessary.

When there is really a conviction that I am only an instrument, like the billions of human beings through which God or Totality functions, how can there not be a tremendous sense of freedom?

Seeking is not a matter of comprehension;
it is a matter of intuitive apprehension.
But it has to be arrived at through the
intellect.

The no-mind state is not the vacancy of
idiocy but the most supremely alert
intelligence, undistracted by extraneous
thought.

The animal does not have to face the kind of problems which oppress man and which are created by the operation of the intellect. An animal's sense of consonance and dissonance, affinity and antipathy is intuitive and in-built as conditioned reflex, rather than subject to the complex interference of ratiocination by which man is not only aware of his perceptions and actions but *also thinks about them.*

Time is only a concept. The future moves into the past leaving no time for the present. When the relativity of time is understood as merely a concept for the measurement of apparent change, then there is only the present moment, which is eternity itself.

Within the whole process of evolution, individuals are really quite irrelevant except as impersonal instruments through which the process itself takes place.

You have considered yourself to be a separate "self" only because of having regarded a "solid" object with a name, that is the body, as yourself. But in fact the body itself is nothing but an insignificant, vastly intricate complex of electrical wave-patterns, a series of rhythmic functions, a throbbing field of energy, and *emptiness*. What you *actually* are, then, is what everybody else is: sentience itself. Therefore, instead of being a puny self by way of an object, you are indeed *everything*.

Fear is really based on the *memory* of past experiences and not on the experiences themselves, because those are *dead*.

Consciousness directs you through the ego to whichever place you're supposed to be.

The intellect must at some stage see that what it is trying to understand is beyond its comprehension, is of a totally different dimension.

It is vital to realize that UNDER-STANDING IS ALL, that there is no question of altering or amending WHAT IS, and that therefore the very question of any method or technique for "attaining" enlightenment is totally irrelevant.

The transcending of thought happens not through suppression but through the natural absence of volition or desire brought about by the recognition of one's true nature.

On the basis of individuality and freedom of choice the manifest universe will never yield its secret.

Our world is not, in fact, an objective world but a purely subjective one, a world of thought, a world of the word, a world given rise to by the extraordinary fertility of the imagination.

Intellect is essential to bring a sentient being to the point of take-off into Self-realization, which is the point where intellect recognizes that it *cannot know its own source.*

The surest signs of spiritual progress are
a lack of concern about spiritual progress
and an absence of anxiety about liberation.

Liberation is only being rid of the idea that
there is anyone who needs liberation.

The entity that is supposed to be reincarnated in another body does not even itself exist except as a concept! How can a mere *concept* be reborn?

It is when the intuitive apprehension of one's true nature is complete that the distinction between knowledge and ignorance becomes irrelevant. Nothing remains as either ignorance or knowledge, and indeed one's very identity has disappeared into formlessness itself.

The usual meaning of worship connotes some kind of reverential bowing in humility, but genuine worship refers to the cessation of conceptual activity in a state of no-mind. Such true worship can only occur spontaneously, and never by volitional effort. Positive or negative efforts toward it can only be a hindrance. Yet, when it comes about spontaneously, its result can be an instantaneous total transformation of the worshiper.

Deeply understanding and accepting that life and living is based on change, whether one likes it or not, is a great step ahead.

The human mind thinks in lateral terms, but almost everything in the universe is circular. Anything that changes has to come back again.

The universe is in continuous movement, yet is always in balance.

Desire refers not only to desiring some object, but even to the desire for enlightenment. The need to know, to have the knowledge of one's true nature, even that is a desire, and that desire is by the "me."

When conceptualizing ceases, the outward false-seeing stops, and what remains is in-seeing, not seeing *inside* but seeing from within as the *source of all seeing*.

Apart from the futility of effort itself, any attempt to prevent thoughts from arising divides the mind artificially into that which does the prevention against that which is being prevented, creating only neurosis and conflict. Whatever thoughts arise (being without substance) will promptly vanish by themselves if they are not accepted and pursued as effective reality. To try to erase thoughts consciously and deliberately is like trying to wash away blood with blood.

❖   ❖   ❖   ❖   ❖

All action is spontaneous, and all volition is an illusion. Once this is realized, one ceases *to try* to be spontaneous. Seeing the falseness of volition makes all action automatically spontaneous.

Our existence is trapped between desire
and fear *in the context of time.* The core of
our problem, then, lies in *thought,* which
is the *creator of time.*

Human beings actually have no more in-
dependence or autonomy in living their
lives than do the characters in a dream.
Neither do they have anything to do with
the creation of the dream or anything in
it. They are simply *being lived* along with
everything else in this living dream of the
manifested universe. The entire dream is
unreal. Only the dreamer is real, and that
is Consciousness itself.

Human beings, whatever they may think, do not live and exercise volition but are *entirely lived.* The importance of an individual life, and even the fact of living itself, has been vastly overestimated and exaggerated. Nature itself defies the human presumption of the "sacredness of life" with the strongest possible demonstration that life is purely incidental to the totality of the manifest, functional order.

All conundrums, all apparent riddles, paradoxes and contradictions subsist only in the split-mind based on subject-object relationship. They resolve themselves as soon as they are seen from the viewpoint of Totality.

Self-realization is not meant for one whose intellect has been deadened by a firm belief in the illusory reality of himself as an entity in the phenomenal world and who thus pursues fulfillment in the illusory pleasures of the senses. Such a person, who has objectivized the phenomenal world in his own mind, does not realize that it is the same illusory mind which destroys both himself and his world. He therefore remains subject to, and victim of, his own notions of birth, suffering and death.

Peace or quietude is always there until the mind intrudes.

Fighting the ego, the mind, is precisely
what the ego wants. You cannot fight the
mind. You cannot suppress the ego.
Fighting, resisting, controlling it is an impossible action. What is really needed is a
negative or feminine action. That is to
yield, to allow things to be as they are.

Knowing that the intrusion of the mind is
a natural process, that it has to happen,
that understanding itself will return one
to the witnessing.

Self-enquiry is the direct path to Self-realization or enlightenment. The only way to make the mind cease its outward activities is to turn it inward. By steady and continuous investigation into the nature of the mind, the mind itself gets transformed into That to which it owes its own existence.

When both the rational and intuitive planes of mind are allowed full operation, they get superimposed on each other resulting in a fasting of the mind or NO-MIND state. This is the most alert state in which the mind can find itself because of the total freedom in which it can operate - a beautiful, natural blending of discipline and spontaneity.

Understanding Nature is not an intellectual exercise but a direct experience in mental silence. Mental silence does not mean keeping the mind dull or empty. Indeed, wordless contemplation can exist coincidentally with thinking when such thinking is witnessed without judgement and therefore without involvement.

Thought is absent in seeing things intuitively. When you perceive directly, there is no thinking. When you think you understand, you don't. You do not *think* that you are alive, you *know* that you are alive.

What begins must end. What appears must disappear. The duration of appearance is a matter of relativity, but the inviolable principle is that whatever is subject to time and duration must end and is therefore not Real.

What is normal may be felt in the silent mind. When thought is spent, the individual is no longer a separate entity but gets merged in the silent Consciousness as its intrinsic essence.

Words must be used like stepping stones: lightly and with nimbleness, because if you step on them too heavily, you incur the danger of falling into the intellectual mire of logic and reason.

To seek life, it must be destroyed: the one seeking real LIFE must himself die.

The ABSOLUTE state cannot be described
because IT is itself the source of all
thought. The shadow cannot know the
substance by which it is cast. The mind
can only *point* towards THAT, and the
irony of it is that *any* direction of pointing
is necessarily away from THAT.

Without consciousness, a body is nothing
but a carcass, and the mind-intellect,
which is the content of consciousness,
must have the keenness to realize its own
strict limitation. Mind has to be treated as
the servant, not the master.

Responsibility and guilt are imaginary
concepts based on the mistaken notion
that a sentient being has independent existence, autonomy and choice of action.
But to think that any individual being can
act independently is itself the basic mistake. Although sentient beings *appear* to
act and react, all functioning really happens *only* in Consciousness.

If one apprehends the total manifestation
with the whole mind and not with the
dichotomized mind of an individual, one
is not far from the Great Awakening. And
then whatever one does is of no importance.

Good and evil, as with all complementary opposites, are merely arbitrary concepts relative to personal, vested interest. What is "good" for one may well be "evil" for another.

If there is no thought, there is no "me", and if there is no "me", there is neither thought nor desire nor fear. The whole intent and purpose of Self-enquiry is to focus the attention intensely and ceaselessly on the sense of "I" so that the spurious imposter "me" and its identifications are exposed as nonexistent.

You cannot deliberately stop worrying. If you try to stop worrying, you get even more involved. So what is the answer? It is simple: when worry comes up, let it come up. As worry comes up, if it is merely witnessed, you are not taken deeper into further involvement.

The human being seeking security in a world which is continuously changing is bound to be frustrated.

There cannot be any volition. God cannot
let two billion people have volition and
still run this universe with any kind of
precision!

The significant point about any sensory
perception, however incredibly quick the
process may be, is that *it still happens in
duration*. Thus, the ineluctable fact is that
our *present* is already the *past* by the time
we experience it, and therefore we cannot
even know the present as such.

Time, the fear of the unknown, and thought which projects what it wants for tomorrow are all bound together in one package that spells conflict, separation and misery.

The mind freed of "me" and its desires is free to move in boundless space with the silent pulse of the universe.

Thoughts just witnessed get cut off for the simple reason that there is no comparing, no judging, no decision making.

Consciousness has produced this play. Consciousness has written the script. Consciousness is playing all the characters. And Consciousness is witnessing the play. It's a one man show.

You ask the questions: "To whom is this happening? Who is concerned? Who wants to know?" The purpose of self-inquiry is to stop the mind from proceeding with the question itself, which is precisely what is meant by witnessing.

At the intellectual level there can be no end to questions. Instead, hang on to the one who is asking. That is all you need do. Indeed, there is nothing else really that you *could* do. If you can do this, never allowing the self to escape your attention, you will ultimately find that the seeker is none other than consciousness seeking its own source and that the seeker himself is both the seeking and the sought - and THAT IS YOU.

To this that you see as the universe, there is no purpose. It is all a *lila*, a play in which we join and contribute some entertainment to pass the time.

Thinking is a pernicious, acquired habit. It is not man's real nature. All that comes out of it is sheer nonsense for the strengthening of the false sense of ego.

What does one want to protect? That without which nothing else has any meaning or value: the *animating presence of Consciousness*, without which you cannot know or enjoy anything. And the best way to protect anything is not to be away from it at all. This is the purpose of spiritual practice - *to remain continuously one with Consciousness all the time.*

There can be no Self-realized *person* because where Self-realization is, the difference between self and others has disappeared and along with it the doership and identity of the individual pseudo-personality.

If hurt is to be avoided and fear overcome,
then the creation of images by the mind
must be arrested.

To accept that the universe is an illusion
without including him who accepts it as
such as *also* being an illusion is a basic
mistake common in spiritual seeking.
When this mistake is seen for what it is,
the seeking will be over.

You will find peace, or rather peace will *find itself,* when there is the apperception that what you are searching for *cannot be found*.

It goes without saying that witnessing can take place only so long as the show goes on, and the show can go on only so long as there is consciousness. So who is to understand all this? Consciousness, of course, understanding itself! There is nothing *but* Consciousness.

What I want to tell you is astoundingly simple if only the listener is totally absent!

People imagine that they must somehow change themselves from imperfect human beings into perfect ones known as sages. The absurdity is that the one thinking along these lines is *himself a fiction.*

To the extent that an individual wishes to experience the world as separate from himself, he is a spectacle without a spectator. To the extent that he prefers to be insensitive to the world, he is a spectator without a spectacle. But it is only when life is accepted totally, however it comes, knowing it to be nothing but a dream yet acting intuitively as if it is real, that one will experience life fully as the natural spectator of the natural spectacle.

There is no gainsaying the fact that Reality or Truth cannot be expressed at all, and in fact there is no need at all to express what is understood - it could only make Truth untrue.

The most that anyone can do in respect to the spiritual search is to keep firmly in mind the essential facts that:

A. The human being has no separate existence apart from the total manifestation;

B. As an individual, he has neither choice nor initiative about the circumstances in which he finds himself;

C. Therefore, any effort or struggle beyond keeping this in mind is fundamentally an exercise in futility.

The truth is that you are neither what you appear to be nor what you think you are. These are mere mental imagery. You are *as yourself* just nothing, and that nothingness which you are is the Consciousness of which the whole universe is the objective body.

To avoid being lost in the bewildering diversity of the play of *maya,* it is necessary to remember the essential unity between the Absolute and the relative, between the Unmanifest and the manifest.

The understanding of Truth is not a matter of time. Indeed, it is prior to the concept of time. When it takes place, it happens suddenly, almost as a shock of timeless apprehension. It means a sudden cessation of the process of duration, a split-second when the functioning of time itself is suspended and integration takes place with what is prior to relativity — direct apprehension of the Absolute.

The pointing by the *guru* to the Truth is like the pointing out of a destination by someone who has already traversed a road and *knows* to where it leads. From this viewpoint he is not only important but necessary. But it is a great error to expect that the *guru* will *carry* the disciple to the destination. This he cannot and will not do.

A true *guru* is concerned not with changing the world or the behavior of the disciple but only with taking the disciple back to the very source of manifestation itself.

The final truth is that ultimate understanding in which there is no comprehender to comprehend the final truth.

It is the natural polarity of interdependent opposites that constitutes the harmony of universal manifestation. The inevitable result of man's attempt to usurp this polarity by egoic self-determination is disharmony, conflict and self-destruction.

It is important to ponder on what you hear, and infinitely more important to ponder on *who* hears it.

Consciousness must first be there before anything else can BE. All inquiry of the seeker of truth must therefore relate to this consciousness, this sense of conscious presence which as such has no personal reference to any individual.

There is an extremely important but subtle aspect of spiritual development that is often lost sight of. It is that in each case, depending on the makeup of each psyche, the development is taking place spontaneously according to nature and that any deliberate efforts on the part of the pseudo-entity only create hazards and obstructions. If this is kept in mind, one automatically evades the greatest spiritual danger, which is the uprising of the ego. What, then, is the individual to do? Merely to let true understanding deeply impregnate his very being, passively and patiently, so that all illusions and obstructions gradually fall off by themselves.

True knowledge can come only when there is total vacancy.

True humility is not the opposite of pride
but the very negation of a separate entity
who could either be *proud or humble*.

The teachings of enlightened Masters attempt to describe the indescribable, to express the inexpressible. The difficulty is
that words can only refer to duality,
whereas their subject in this case is THAT
in which there is no duality whatsoever.

The Sages, men of vision, have never asked anyone to believe *anything*. Belief is nothing but concept. The Sages have always merely pointed at the Truth, which the disciple must then *realize* himself.

Man lives in constant fear that the happiness achieved in one moment may disappear in the next. He hopes for constant, changeless joy without realizing that continuous change is the essence of phenomenal existence and that so long as he thinks and acts as an independent entity he will be relentlessly subjected to the lacerations of time.

It is the false sense of separation between man's fictional personal identity and the rest of the world that is the cause of all human conflict and unhappiness. Yet, with unbelievable obtuseness, man still seeks salvation only from this imaginary unhappiness rather than from the false identity that is its cause!

Our imperfect perception of the manifested world in terms of measurement, diversification and classification is the veil that maintains our commitment to illusion.

What we call our voluntary actions are in fact involuntary, and our supposed personal free-will is nothing but an ineffectual and temporary obstruction to the natural, involuntary workings of the universe. But even our false assumption of volition is as involuntary as everything else and can only fall off when we have involuntarily seen it as false.

Making positive effort to stop thinking as a spiritual practice is an exercise in futility, and so is any other kind of effort. The only effective effort is instant apperception of truth, which is in fact effortless.

The word "surrender" is used where there is a duality between "me" and God. When this surrender happens, this will which we think of as ours drops off, and there is total acceptance that all that prevails is His Will.

It is impossible for the human intellect to understand the working of the universe.

However much we think and believe that we're living our own lives, the fact of the matter is that our lives are being lived.

When you stop searching and let the impersonal consciousness take over, then it lets you in on the mystery of its own source, and you will know that *things have no substance*.

All problems are created because we think, we conceptualize, we fabricate symbols and images, including images of ourselves. But no image has any actual substance, and if this conceptualization stops by being seen for what it really is, an astounding change cannot but take place.

The subjective feeling of presence of a man who lives a few decades, an insect who lives for a few days, or a tortoise who lives for a few centuries is in no way different.

Along with keen intellect one must have *faith* in order to grasp the basic essentials of truth. And that faith must be of the kind that can accept the *guru's* words as God's own truth. Faith is the first step, and no further progress is possible until the first step is taken.

What is it that one loves most? Is it not this "I am", the conscious presence which one wants to preserve at any cost? *I AM itself is God*.

There is no such thing as a Self-realized person. A person does not remain a person after Self-realization.

Through knowledge you can only pretend to know Truth. True knowledge is freedom from knowledge itself after it has disappeared into the vacancy of a fasting mind.

The sage is indifferent. He does not hanker after more pleasure, nor does he refuse whatever may come to him by way of experience. There is no volition, either positive or negative, because there is no separate entity to choose, want or strive for anything.

Man, unaware of the seamless unity of all things, pulls in one direction and in turn finds himself pulled helplessly in the opposite direction. He considers himself superior to his environment and yet is ignorant even of the origin of his own thoughts. He does not truly know whether any action of his is really of his own volition or predetermined. He thinks he can shape his own destiny and yet is piteously anxious about his future. He does not realize that his confusion lies within, in the knotted, convoluted tangle of his own conceptualization, and not in outside conditions.

Any reality that can be conceived by an individual entity is based on a belief of personal absoluteness in temporality which is a complete misapprehension in itself. The individual human just cannot accept the fact that his individuality and, more importantly, his individual volition or free-will is nothing more than an illusion.

There is a single, immanent Reality which is at once the source, the substratum and the true nature of everything that is manifested as the universe. This indivisible Reality is directly experienced by every sentient being as the subjective awareness of self, the consciousness of existing and being present.

You cannot "shop" for truth. Truth cannot be seen. What is necessary is a different seeing, *whole seeing,* seeing from within, from the Source of all seeing.

No one is born and no one dies. This dream-world of phenomena is merely something to be witnessed in passing.

Tortured and stultified by the utter failure of his intellect to grasp the ultimate reality, man has conceptualized God in the *image of himself* attributing to it the noblest sentiments and qualities he himself wants but lacks. To reach that which is beyond this God, the transcendent and immanent ground of all manifestation, the intellect is powerless. There is no path to that which is timeless and present everywhere and which is itself the source of all thought.

Living through sequential time, with its pains and losses, remorse and regrets, combined with the hopes and fears of the future, constitutes an unbelievable load of suffering that we accept as the "normal" condition only because we are so used to our false identity as a separate bodily entity. The total surrender of this burden is absolute freedom.

Once the spontaneity of the whole process of manifestation in its totality is apprehended and the hollowness of the distinction between "self" and "other" is realized, there cannot possibly be any more question of a separate individual who can either be "born" or "die."

Our phenomenal world is not a collection of entities. It is *one total process* in which things, including human beings, are not objects but *events*.

The final truth is simple: all things exist in Consciousness, all things flow from Consciousness, all things ARE Consciousness because *Consciousness is all there is.*

When events correspond with what we consider agreeable, we take pride in our "personal achievement." When they do not, we are frustrated. But everything we take to be the result of our volition is in fact only the inevitable.

Self, experienced in the egoless state, is
the supreme Reality.

✧   ✧   ✧   ✧   ✧

My relative absence is my absolute presence. The moment of death will be the
moment of highest ecstasy, the last senso-
rial perception of the psychosomatic apparatus.

Stand in your original state of wholeness, the state before you were born when there was no knowledge "I am" and therefore no need or want of any kind. All suffering will end as soon as you stand in pure Awareness.

Intellect is very much necessary to understand certain fundamentals, but there is a strict limit beyond which it cannot go. Thereafter it is only when intellect gives up all efforts and acknowledges total surrender that intuition takes over. Awakening can only happen spontaneously by itself.

Did you find any need for knowledge a hundred years ago? That which you do not know and cannot know is your true state.

Our entire life seems to be nothing but a wasted effort to control our natural responses and reactions to events and change them to suit what we think are our preferred requirements. Yet, the controller himself is nothing more than a *concept* created by thought, by memory, by the past.

There are many reports of what are popularly considered "death-experiences", which are mistaken as evidence of what happens after death. These are in fact only hallucinations experienced by the ego arising from stimulation of certain centers of the brain *before*, not *after*, the completion of the death process. Most of the mystical phenomena recorded as yogic experience are of the same order, movements in consciousness experienced by the ego. But when man finally surrenders his miserable egoic individuality, there is no experience of anything. *He is the Totality itself.*

It is *wanting* that is the cause of bondage, irrespective of whether that wanting is for some material benefit or for realization. Man's viewpoint has become so inverted that he thinks of effortless, unfathomable contentment as an *abnormal* condition that must be *attained* through *want* by some special positive "spiritual" efforts!

In true dialogue neither the query nor the answer has any dialectic basis because only the *heart* is concerned and not the mind.

From beyond the parameters of all inter-related opposites the *guru* mysteriously uses the persona of duality to express love without any apparent relationship. His work is at a level prior to the conceiving of any level at all! In other words, it is conceptually impossible to comprehend what the *guru* is.

We speak of diversity in the manifest world as of water in a mirage. Time, space and duality itself are all notions or concepts—mere thoughts. All is nothing but Consciousness appearing as mind, whether mountains, oceans, rivers, animals or human beings.

The true *guru* is not hiding anything of the Truth. He is the very source of knowledge, indeed the knowledge itself, and everyone is free to take away as much as he can. There is no question of any personal giving or receiving because no individual ever did exist.

Understand that there is nothing warrant-
ing reverence or religious awe in the
spontaneous process of manifestation.

The life of a sage appears to others to be
as purposeless as the actions of an infant.
The infant lives in the bliss of ignorance,
while the self-realized sage lives in the
bliss beyond both ignorance and knowledge. In fact the sage is no longer even an
individual, in spite of the presence of a
fully developed intellect.

Where human relations are concerned, force can only defeat itself because every action must produce a reaction, every challenge a corresponding resistance, in a never-ending chain of cause-effect relationship. Every event or action that tends to alter the existing position produces a resistance, and without alteration of the existing position there is no event or action.

The *guru* does nothing more than negate the disciple as an entity while at the same time negating himself as the *guru*.

The crux of man's dilemma lies in the concept of time. While chasing his mythical happiness of the future, man has no time to enjoy the present moment. And actually there is no such thing as the present because by the time one thinks of it, it has already become the past. Therefore, what is vital is not *thinking* about the present but actually *being* the present moment — and that is nothing other than enlightenment.

One hammer blow after another is usually needed to destroy the sense of duality. Once duality cracks open and the essential Unicity is understood in its entirety, the whole-mind starts functioning, and there is utter joy because *no aspect* of bondage survives this understanding, not even the concept of bondage and freedom.

We do not really live but are being *lived*.
There is nothing anywhere but the one
universal, impersonal "I", and not a single object anywhere has any existence independent of it.

Once the body dies, manifested consciousness is released and merges with
the impersonal Consciousness like a drop
of water merges with the ocean. No individual identity survives death.

You may believe that this whole universe is a dream and all the human beings mere dreamed characters within that dream, but so long as you yourself remain outside that dream and view it as an individual, separate from it, you cannot approach closer to the Truth.

Truth consists in being aware of WHAT IS without thinking about it.

The whole cosmos is an implicit unity
expressed in explicit duality. The original
interrelated opposites are beingness and
non-beingness. Being can only come out
of non-being, precisely as sound only
emanates from silence and light from
darkness. The imagined void of non-
being, however, is not emptiness but the
very fullness of potential out of which
arises all that exists.

All events must take their noumenally
determined course, consistent or inconsistent, and whether the person concerned in them is a self-realized sage or
not. An ordinary individual, however,
will feel gratified or frustrated while the
sage remains always totally unconcerned.

The man who embraces the world as real, like the man embracing a woman in his dream, ultimately awakens to find nothing there but himself.

In the absence of intention there can be no psychological basis for any involvement with activity and events or their outcome. There is then perfect alignment with whatever might happen, an acceptance of events without any feeling of either achievement or frustration.

The beginning of inner transformation is a deep feeling of utter dissatisfaction with life, otherwise called *dispassion*. This is the point of the inward turning of personal consciousness. It is the point of no return in the quest for life's source.

With realization, or the apperception of WHAT IS, the existence of the physical body ceases to be relevant. The psychosomatic mechanism will then exist for the rest of its life merely as a part of the totality of functioning without any illusion of personal volition.

Only in the absolute absence of all conceptualization is to be found the perfect peace
of Absolute Presence.

The only true meditation is the constant
impersonal witnessing of all that takes
place in one's life as mere movements in
the universal Consciousness.

The *guru* who helps you escape from sorrow by prescribing procedures and methods is *not* an enlightened *guru*. A true sage requires that you *face* your sorrow so thoroughly and intimately that it disappears in the very understanding of itself.

The ordinary way of seeing is totally inadequate. A very special kind of seeing is needed for comprehending Reality, an intuitive seeing wherein it is seen that there is nothing to be seen and no one to see it.

Don't try to do anything out of the ordinary. Don't try to amend your way of life. Don't try to alter your way of life. Don't deliberately add anything. Don't deliberately subtract anything. Just carry on as you have been doing. What could be simpler than that?

Instead of getting involved in a mental process, it is simpler and more effective to remain in a position of joyous acceptance. A thought has come, it is witnessed, and it gets cut off. The witnessing does not need any mental processes.

You are not an individual being, let alone
an individual doer. You're not even an
individual entity! You are nothing. You
are merely a pattern of vibrating energy.
Truly understanding that, with conviction, will help tremendously.

The joke is that it is the ego, the "me," that
wants enlightenment, and enlightenment
cannot come until the "me" is demolished.

Give one little chance to His will and see
what happens. I think you will be surprised.

The subject of TRUTH is without substance, yet so very full and pregnant that
no other subject has any value in comparison to it.

A mirror can only reflect all things by virtue of the fact that in itself it contains nothing and retains nothing. Thus, neither can Consciousness ever be anything objective, for it is the mirror on which all objective phenomenality is projected and without which there is nothing.

Transformation cannot be brought about, it can only *happen*. Indeed, practicing meditation is itself bondage! Transformation presupposes the total absence of any *doer* practicing *anything*.

The disciple goes to the *guru* seeking enlightenment as something which he can enjoy as an individual, while the enlightened *guru* knows their relationship to be a completely impersonal evolutionary process in which no individuals figure at all.

Volitional action has no more relation to events as their cause than the crowing of a rooster does to the rising of the sun.

All our struggles are like the frustrated flutterings of a caged bird - they make no difference.

The universe is not the universal Consciousness, but Consciousness IS the universe, just as the bracelet is made of gold, but the gold is not made of the bracelet.

Events happening through any body-mind mechanism are always beyond the control of that entity.

He who believes that he has choice of decision and action continues to be miserable.

The sage doesn't reconcile discipline with understanding or combine order with spontaneity. It just happens, and therein lies the magic and wonder of it.

When adaptability toward living with others and the desire to have one's own individual life are seen as opposites and conflicting, there's misery. But when it is understood that both work spontaneously together, then there is an automatic, natural order of conciliation between them.

Pleasure for the Sage is more intense because he's not worrying about when he'll have it again. If it comes again, fine; if not, it doesn't bother him.

When there is only witnessing and no witness, the split-mind is reunited as whole-mind into which the ego disappears along with the affliction of volition. Mind dissolves the absence, and what remains is our true nature in all its pristine radiance.

To consider that the world has no meaning or purpose is merely to say that the world is not centered on humanity. Without his ideals and motivations, an individual is frightened of being a nothing in the nothingness of a purposeless world. In actuality, man's ideals of "purpose" as the basis of life and nature are nothing but his own conditioned concepts. Nature cannot be seen in terms of human thought, logic or language. What appears cruel and unjust in nature seems so only when the matter is considered from the viewpoint of a separated and estranged individual human. But the rest of nature is totally unconcerned because the rest of nature is not human-hearted.

The original and eternal state of ours can no more be described than can the state of deep sleep. What spills over into the description is the sense of peace and contentment, but the state itself cannot be defined. Beyond merely pointing at it, words can only turn into silence.

Religions were originally based on direct or absolute Truth. In the course of time they degenerated into concepts. And on these concepts has been erected gradually an enormous, amorphous structure enchanting enough to attract and mislead millions of people.

The surest sign of spiritual progress is a total lack of concern about progress. There is an utter absence of anxiety about anything like liberation and a sort of hollowness in one's being, a kind of looseness and involuntary surrender to whatever might happen.

Nothing is single, nothing is constant, nothing. Everything is changing all the time. Change and the polarity of interconnected opposites are the very core of phenomenal existence.

There can be no technique or system for that total transformation in viewpoint called enlightenment for the simple reason that all effort must necessarily emanate from the illusory ego, that very mind of thought-intellect which has brought about the sorry plight from which the individual seeks freedom.

In the mechanics of intellect, conceptualization is a process where only one part of the mental operation is favored, not just by ignoring the other part but by specifically rejecting it. We have thus become so conditioned to accept the rational intellect and reject wild intuition that we feel ourselves enslaved by nature, whereas it is not nature that enslaves us but our attachment to our particular interpretation of it. We forget that nature is not different from us - *we are nature.* Indeed, it is this separation from the rest of nature that we ourselves create which is the cause of all our conflict both within and without and of our wanton destruction of nature itself.

The fear of death is actually a product of the desire to perpetuate one's identity. Were you not dead before you were born? Those who know Reality know the falsehood of life and death.

Normal thinking and speech are the result not of unconscious habit but of a definite partiality for convergent thinking. Convergent thinking affords an apparent sense of safety and meaningfulness as against the undesirable abnormality and threatening meaninglessness of the divergent mind. Divergent thinking defies logic and reason by establishing inconsistent connections and anomalous analogies between cabbages and kings. But the result of this lopsided partiality is our world of duality which is in constant contradiction with itself and which prevents us from seeing Reality.

The human condition in terms of good and evil, which really means pleasure and pain, is like that of fleas on a hot griddle - he who jumps must fall, and he who falls must jump.

On the surface it seems unacceptable that
one's efforts to understand and realize the
Truth cannot be successful without the
help and grace of someone else, namely
the *guru*. But this is because the seeker
regards himself as a separate, autonomous individual and the *guru* as another
individual with a similarly separate existence. As long as this attitude prevails,
however, whatever else one does to attain
liberation will not only be utterly useless
but will result in a tightening of one's
bondage. Why so? Because what one
thinks one is as an independent entity is
actually nothing but a fleeting shadow in
the imagination. So long as there is a "me"
thinking and reacting as an entity, the
seeker will continue going around and
around like a dog chasing his tail and
remain inaccessible to the help or grace of
the *guru*.

Self-realization is not only effortless, it is
effortlessness itself.

M A Y 5

The dispassion which is at the root of true spiritual seeking is neither the dulling of the senses through an excess of sensual enjoyment nor the suppression of the senses through forced disciplines. Both these lead only to frustration and confusion. It is only *after* sufficient sensory experience that a sense of dispassion can arise through realization that life and living *must* have a deeper meaning than the mere pleasures or paths of sensory experience. *Then* the genuine seeking begins.

The past is dead memory, and the future is nonexistent. The present moment is *not between* the future and the past, but the *constant dimension outside of time.*

MAY 6

One cannot but laugh and even be apparently irreverent when confronted by the fantastic superstructure of superstition and mystery that has been built on and around the basic simplicity that TRUTH is!

That this entire phenomenal show of the universe has no purpose indicates the obvious futility of seeking a goal in life. No sooner is a goal conceived than spontaneity is at once destroyed and the self-conscious ego takes over in destructive competition against everything that comes, thus missing all that is worthwhile in life. It is, indeed, the "purposeful" life which entirely misses out on the purpose of life! The true purposeless vision misses nothing and enjoys everything without inhibition.

Man has himself created the horrific problems which face him today. For hundreds of years man has been trying to "improve" the world, and if there is chaos as he sees it, it is only he himself who is responsible. It is presumptuous beyond measure for the individual human with his puny brain, donated by the courtesy of nature, to have arrogated to himself proprietorship over the whole natural order. We have, in fact, so separated ourselves from the universe and its unimaginably complex system of relationships that the more we try to control the world, the faster it runs away from us. It is only when the individual can view the universe as inseparable from himself that he sees everything in its true perspective. Technology becomes destructive wherever this oneness of the universe is not understood. Most significant, however, is that man's very misunderstanding of the universe is also a necessary aspect of WHAT IS in the inevitable functioning of Totality!

❖   ❖   ❖   ❖   ❖

The significance of true philosophy is that it works - in the sense that its strength lies not in its words but in the active practice of it.

The ego naturally fears the inevitability of death because it means its own destruction. Yet deep down, man always knows with intuitive conviction that he is really immortal, and it is for this reason that he is always seeking, consciously or unconsciously, his true nature.

At a certain level of magnification the various cells of an organism appear to be engaged in a fierce and ruthless battle for individual survival. Yet if the organism as a whole is observed at a different level of magnification, it is clearly seen that what appears as conflict at the lower level is indeed harmony at the higher level. And so it is with the ceaseless flow of energy passing through infinitely diverse patterns, expressing the rhythm and unity of Life throughout the changing myriads of forms in the manifest universe, for which the illusory individual ego has unnecessarily and mistakenly assumed the burden of concern.

For any event to happen an object is needed. So, when enlightenment is about to happen a body-mind organism is created in this evolution which is ready to receive that enlightenment. It is given the characteristics — physical, mental, temperamental — which make that body-mind organism capable of receiving enlightenment.

If the mind watches its own operation, then there will always be comparing and judging: "This is good, this is bad, this is whatever." That is not witnessing.

Life can be really and truly simple if we
don't fight it.

In one's natural, immediate attention or
awareness there are no boundaries, no
separate items of manifestation, unless
and until thought intrudes and directs specific concentration on a particular thing.
And this is what creates separation along
with the whole chain of other thoughts and
reactions that lead to every kind of conflict and unhappiness, which we then interpret as bondage. But the realization
that boundaries are a product of thought
is at once the realization that the separation caused by these boundaries and the
conflicts that ensue are *all* an illusion.

Nature does not know or care about the world of man-made opposites. Nature is perfectly satisfied and happy to produce a world of infinite, rapturous variety that knows nothing about pretty or ugly, ethical or unethical. Nature never apologizes for anything, nor does it see or acknowledge anything of man's misconceived errors of opposition.

Man has become addicted to the drug named "intellect" and under its influence compulsively analyzes everything, cogitating, speculating and making all simple things complicated. This addiction can only be gotten rid of by unconditional surrender to the process of pure receptivity.

What prevents the natural interpenetration between the individual and the outer world is fear, and fear alone - the horror of being gobbled up and totally annihilated by the ever-present specter of death. But when the whole panorama of manifestation, *including the one who experiences it,* is seen to be but a mirror-imaging in consciousness of the subjective REALITY, where is death or anyone to fear it?

Seeking the source of the "me" does not mean replacing one set of thoughts for another but getting rid of all thoughts by fixing the attention on that Self which is the *constant presence behind the mind.*

If any individual considers himself enlightened, then he is not. The precondition of enlightenment is that the identified individual self has been annihilated. No personal self or individual phenomenon has *ever* been enlightened. The person disappears along with all other phenomena when he awakens from this dream of existence.

Our lives are in fact being lived for us rather than by us as we seem to think. All our experience, if carefully analyzed, would clearly show that volition is really not a significant factor in our lives. Only the most minute fraction of our total physical and mental functioning even appears to be subject to volition. Did you exercise volition when you were conceived? And when the conceived material grew in the mother's womb? How long can you live without sleep, without food or water? How long can you go without the excretory movements of the body? How do you breathe and digest your food? Do you have the absolute certainty of remaining alive for even the next five minutes on the strength of your own volition?

In order to understand this strange, un-known, starkly inevitable thing called death we must first understand life. What we must find out is *what we are now*.

❖   ❖   ❖   ❖   ❖

You are not the mind. It is axiomatic that the perceiver cannot be the perceived. You can perceive your body; therefore, you are not the body. You can perceive your thoughts; therefore, you are not the mind. That which cannot be perceived or conceived is what you ARE.

The sense of LOVE which is the essence of Consciousness gets turned into love for material objects when Consciousness identifies with the things it manifests. This attachment toward things of the world falls off only when there is clear understanding of our True Nature.

The identified man takes part in things and suffers. The unidentified man merely watches the spectacle. The identified man tries to *understand* truth while the unidentified man *experiences* it.

True prayer means not solicitation but *communion.* Prayer is communion in the same sense as that in true meditation there is neither a meditator nor anything meditated upon.

To die *now* to every moment and every experience is the death that is ETERNITY ITSELF.

There is no need to avoid false thoughts
or seek true ones because *all* thought is
spontaneous, involuntary and without
substance. It is neither to be accepted nor
rejected but *ignored* so that it disappears
as spontaneously as it appeared.

For the sage there is no illusion of the
manifest universe at all, and there is therefore no question of the duality called relationship, male/female, good/bad or
otherwise. He moves through life as if it
is real but never gets involved because his
mind is always whole.

By being constantly and effortlessly *aware* of life without *thinking* about it, this awareness soon continues to function even when there are thoughts floating through the mind just as clouds floating through the sky leave no change in the space.

No action or process, the basis of which is duration, could possibly bring about a suspension in its own temporal functioning. Awakening is an instantaneous break in the succession of duration which can only come about through an intuitive apprehension of immediate timelessness.

Experienced in the egoless state, Self is the supreme Reality. But self-enquiry is not an intellectual process, and no amount of thinking about self-enquiry is itself self-enquiry.

For the liberated mind, death is realized as the unknown potential from which has arisen the birth and life itself. The event of death is seen as just another moment in life, complete and unknown until it arrives.

Essentially, what the average person wants out of life is just one thing: happiness. It is in this quest that he goes through life day after day in the firm belief that he will somehow, someday find final satisfaction through the things and circumstances of his world. There comes a time, however, when man gets utterly tired, physically and mentally, of this constant search because he finds that it *never ends*. He comes to the startling discovery that every kind of satisfaction has within itself the roots of pain and torment. At this stage his search cannot but take the turn inwards toward that happiness which is independent of external things.

When you are dead, you will be back in the primordial state of rest which existed before you were born, that stillness before all experience. It is only the false sense of a limited, separate "me" that deprives life of its meaning and gives death an ominous significance which it really does not have.

Just as one's dream in sleep exists no-
where but in the mind (both as cause and
effect) so does the universe exist only in
the mind of infinite Consciousness.

It must be constantly borne in mind while
trying to understand the mechanics of the
apparent process of manifestation that
nothing has actually been created. All that
appears is mind-stuff, that of which all
dreams are made, and apart from Consciousness itself, nothing exists, neither
the mind nor the senses nor their objects.

The question of whether a *guru* is really necessary only assumes real significance from the point of view of the impersonal totality of manifestation. From that standpoint both *guru* and disciple are equally necessary to bring about the phenomenon known as enlightenment.

As soon as the Truth is realized, the process of self-destruction which is personal existence is transformed into immortality.

In spite of a certain degree of intellectual understanding, most seekers find it very difficult to accept the total abolition of their personal identities. They continue to work hard at their disciplinary practices hoping for a personal liberation - a contradiction in terms because liberation presupposes the absolute absence of the individual entity.

Every sensory and conceptual experience is an illusion. What you see, hear, touch, smell and taste is really the Unmanifest, the *within* of the without with which we are surrounded on all sides.

One who has become enamored with the song within, one who is united with the inner universal pulse, such a one has become immune to the buffeting of the storms of circumstance without.

In true acceptance of the will of God, there is no *acceptor* at all. Ultimate understanding can only be pure silence. There is no question of any "one" understanding anything or accepting anything.

From the beginning *nothing is*. There really has never been any beginning, nor is there any end. The universe is a dream. *So is the one who is supposed to understand this!* Belief in oneself is, in fact, the only real obstruction to awakening from delusion.

The Earth is but an infinitesimal fraction of the enormous illusion of the universe, not to speak of a mere *person*. Yet, by identifying yourself with such a minute phenomenon as a body-mind organism with a personal sense of doership, you have forfeited your identity with the infinite Totality.

The entire manifested creation presents a cosmic dance by the Divine Dancer, executed to the tune of time on the stage of space, *and the dance cannot be differentiated from the dancer.*

It is the wish to experience life as a separate entity that turns the outer world into a threatening multiple enemy.

You as the knower of the body and the mind are apart from both. You as BE-INGNESS are that which *always is*, irrespective of body and mind.

We consider ourselves to be the presence only of what we appear to be, but what we appear to be is only the costume, the persona put on by what lies underneath. We are the presence of an absence we are unable to perceive and of which we know nothing. So we call it a 'void', and we avoid it.

The limitations of words are clearly seen when they try to remind the Absolute of its true nature. Being merely the expression of thought, they can neither expose ignorance, which is nonexistent, nor reveal the Absolute to which they owe their existence. For this purpose words are as useless as a lamp at midday, which can neither dispel the darkness that is not there nor reveal the light of the sun.

How do you see yourself? You see your body, or rather a part of it, and identify yourself with it. The appearance of your body in consciousness is perceived and interpreted by you exactly as it is done by any other observer. Your own interpretation of yourself is as ephemeral and illusory as that of others (though maybe a little more flattering). But any thought about yourself, whether your own or someone else's, is only a temporary mental image. The solid personality you think yourself to be is nothing more than a flimsy succession of these images stored in the memory. As a person, that is all that you are. But *is that truly you*?

The only thing you know as a matter of certainty is the fact I AM. But you do not know who this "I" is. One must first find out precisely who or what it is that is seeking truth and happiness before there is any possibility of knowing the transcendental Reality.

Just as the difference between the space in a pot and the space outside it disappears when the pot is demolished, so also does duality disappear when it is realized that the difference between the individual consciousness and the Universal Consciousness does not in fact exist.

One does not experience suffering - one suffers an experience. One who is aware of his true identify does not, and cannot, suffer.

Everything has its place in the world as well as in our daily routine. Devotion and reverence are all right, for example, so long as one recognizes them for what they are - affectivity - and to that extent a form of bondage. But when one sees something for what it Is, it then loses its force and cannot effect any further bondage.

It is precisely for the reason that Truth
is utterly simple, basic, elementary and
totally obvious, that it is completely
overlooked.

All things are conditions of mind. That
which knows the mind is the unconditional SELF of everything.

All the causes of human confusion and discontent - desire, greed, envy, anger, pride, fear, etc. - are not independent phenomena but merely the various manifestations of the identified ego. And the great joke is that the identified 'me' wants to be free of these things to 'enjoy' that enlightenment which cannot come about except by the annihilation of that very 'me'!

To understand that our real nature *has no needs* is the only true renunciation.

The individual cannot decide independently, as by choice, that he wants to be liberated, although he may well *think* he has done so. This is where the physical and mental makeup of each psychosomatic apparatus comes in: each one *cannot help but* develop precisely according to the way it is constructed by Nature, whether in the material field or in the spiritual. There is no choice involved whatsoever.

Once it is seen that volition is not only unnecessary but *illusory*, it becomes obvious that in order to see something which is already there no effort is valid. Effort to realize Truth is futile because Truth is all there is. Everything IS Truth. One must abandon the cleverness of reason for bewilderment, which is *intuition* or reliance on the innate principle of BEING.

What the mystic sees is really very simple to understand, but it needs a special kind of intelligence and a special perspective - not an intensified intellect but a kind of *transmuted* intellect which can offer a totally different perspective by transferring to a standpoint beyond itself.

For the egoic being the outer world is seen as the face of an enemy. The disruptive dualism from which all conflict arises is not in the outer world but within the false perception of the pseudo-entity who fails to see the world as his own reflection.

Spontaneous, true action happens naturally when there is no "you" checking whether the action conforms to your own idea of what's best for you.

Human beings have no independent or autonomous existence whether they accept the fact or not. And whether they like it or not, they are being helplessly lived within the vast totality of an imponderably intricate creation over which they have absolutely no control.

Just as a forest conflagration (itself a single body of flame) assumes innumerable forms, so does the formless, nondual Consciousness assume all forms that compose the universe.

The *guru* is a great mystery to whom neither criteria nor inferences of any nature can apply. He is, indeed, the objective expression of the Absolute, living beyond all sense of duality, and cannot, therefore, be factually regarded as an object of worship. He is not an object but *all* objects, including the worshipper.

The void that is REALITY is THAT which is devoid of any *concept* of reality.

The very effort to see into one's own nature is the obstruction to it.

Dispassion means much more than just lack of interest. It means to be seated in the Self, in the infinite intemporality from where continuous, impartial witnessing of all the movements in Consciousness takes place. It is a totally different dimension from the duality in space and time.

Wherever there is desire there is suffering. Liberation can only occur when desire has been totally absent. It is not attainable by any means or effort, which itself depends on desire.

Whatever is sensorially perceived is like
the wrapper of the real thing, a sample, a
description, an advertisement, a mask,
merely the seemingly real outward appearance of what lies behind. Reality is
therefore not the presence but the absence, not the positive but the negative,
not the seen phenomena but their unseen
source, not the known actual but the unknown potential.

Excessive verbal communication has become so compulsive and widespread that
it is taken for granted as the only way to
understand anything. But real Understanding is of a different dimension altogether.

An infant, not being aware of having an individual identity, has no intellect with which to conceptualize and therefore lives in spontaneous freedom without resistance from moment to moment. The same is true of the self-realized sage, who has gone beyond the mind.

One need only float with the magnificent current of Totality in the ecstasy of oneness with the cosmic flow of events. What else can the dreamer do with his dream except passively witness it without judgement?

With the destruction of the body, the ego is also destroyed. It is not and cannot be otherwise because that consciousness which created the individual through identification with a specific body has now merged with the impersonal universal Consciousness.

Since one was not concerned with the phenomenon of one's birth, why should one be concerned with the phenomenon of death? Indeed, there really is no ONE who need be concerned with anything. It is only this very concern, in fact, that constitutes one's bondage as a personal entity.

Understanding is all, and any *effort* to
understand is an obstruction to it. The
impasse disappears when the ego recognizes that it is strangulated in its own trap.
The ego is annihilated by being exposed
as the illusion it is, and this itself is the
Understanding.

When the seeds of thought and conceptualization are burnt to ash by pure Knowledge, there is liberation from the dream
we call waking.

When you listen not to the superficial meaning of words of Truth but in such a way that the listener in you disappears along with the speaker, then the real meaning of the words can sink in deep and your misunderstanding will disappear by itself. There is nothing else to be done.

Until the storm of conceptual thinking subsides and the mind learns to rest in a fasting state, one's true nature must remain unknown and inaccessible.

The misery and unhappiness of the individual human being is due entirely to his ignoring of the basic fact of the universe, which is UNITY.

Man's tragic predicament derives from the fact that thought and its processes have become excessively developed to the exclusion of intuition, so much so that every person confidently thinks of himself as an individual figure exclusive even of the very ground of nature!

The outside world is not really concerned at all in man's dilemma of suffering. It is all within the fictitious 'me' of personal identity. Realization of this fact *is* the ultimate Understanding.

In every moment the totality of function is in perfect balance. Everything IS PERFECTION in every moment - *here and now forever.*

When personal identification vanishes, all that then remains is a sense of presence without the person, which gets translated into a feeling of life as *total freedom*.

The ultimate understanding can come neither by straining to hang on to the material pleasures of the world nor by making efforts to seek and grasp the infinite Absolute. It comes by *recognizing* that the universe is the objective body of the subjective SELF.

It is destiny that determines all that happens including the arising of dispassion that leads to self-enquiry, the meeting between the *guru* and the disciple, *and* the fructifying or otherwise of the *guru's* teaching in the disciple.

Life has to be lived *as if* it is real, while deep down one must know that life is merely *being lived* as an impersonal, phenomenal functioning of universal Consciousness.

What people call realization or enlightenment *already exists* - it is not 'something' to be *acquired*. Therefore, any and every attempt to 'attain' it is an exercise in self-defeating futility.

There is no difference between ignorance and enlightenment as long as there is a conceptual entity to experience either condition.

Realization of the intrinsic inseparability of oneself and everything is emancipation. One is released from solitary confinement in the prison of 'self' into the total freedom of universal identity.

When the qualities of mind are lost, the essentials of the Infinite take over. When the mind vacates, there is pure, infinite Consciousness.

Direct experience of the Self is known as
Self-realization. This is often misunder-
stood to mean that there is a *separate
individual* who is to have knowledge of
the Self. The state of Self-awareness does
not come about until the notion of a separate individual has been totally erased
and the subject-object relationship has
ceased to exist in a direct subjective
awareness of the one indivisible Reality.

What is born must in due course die. The
objective body will thereafter be dissolved and irrevocably annihilated. What
was once a sentient being will be destroyed, never to be reborn. But the consciousness is not objective, not a *thing* at
all. Therefore, consciousness is neither
born nor dies, and certainly cannot be
'reborn'.

When the divine relationship between the guru as Consciousness and the disciple as Consciousness becomes ripe enough to fructify, they meet like two empty mirrors facing each other.

If you give up identification with the body, if you remain quietly absorbed in the sense of Totality, in the I AMness without attachment, you will know all that is to be known.

The primal substance of all beings is the same noumenon. Enlightenment is the name given to the noumenal state. There is no kind of intentional practice, action or effort that can lead an individual to his enlightenment because any intentional deed is based on the superstition that an individual exists apart from the noumenon.

Although it can be seen, the universe is nonetheless purely conceptual and has no actual substance or reality of its own. All phenomena are nonexistent by nature. Other than the primal Absolute subjectivity in which all exists, nothing in fact *does* exist!

To cease fabricating objects in the mind is to stop perceiving what we are not and to apperceive what we ARE.

'Me' is the conceptual flow of time to the future from the past, a flow that makes the relative present impossible to exist, while that which I AM is the eternal present moment.

In the mistaken belief that one is an entity separate from all other people and all other manifestation, *there is no escape from sorrow.*

The individual does not finally *merge* with his original nature any more than a wave merges with water. They were not different to begin with. A wave is nothing more than the shifting shape of the water itself. It is not a question of joining separate things but of the abandonment of something inessential and superficial, the false identity of a separate individual entity.

By knowing what is *not,* the sage knows
what he truly IS.

Polarity, which modern science confirms
as existing in all manifestations of life
even in the most minute atomic and sub-
atomic particles of the universe, is an expression of an intimacy of love that cannot
be described in words.

Silence doesn't mean not talking. Silence is silence of the mind. Silence is absence of questions, absence of thinking, true meditation.

When the inquiring mind, intellectually creating problems, gradually comes to the understanding that the more problems it creates the more veils it creates between the Self and the understanding, then there is silence.

There is no best path or worst path. There is just the path to which each individual organism gets directed.

Love, not as an expression of separateness based on emotion, but as *compassion*, is that which holds the world together in Unicity. In Unicity we do not love others, we ARE them.

One cannot but carry on with that which
is false until it drops off by itself.

To live naturally is to live as a mere witness,
without control and therefore without
mentation, want or volition, uninvolved in
the dream-play of life and living.

The guru does not talk to individuals. He is Consciousness talking about Consciousness to Consciousness.

No truth remains as truth the moment it is given expression. It then becomes only a concept! Is it any wonder, then, that you find yourself bogged down in a mire of ideas and concepts from which you find it impossible to extricate yourself?

The least effort on your part prevents what otherwise might happen naturally and spontaneously. Awareness cannot be an act of volition.

See the false as false, and what remains is true. What is absent now will appear when what is now present disappears. Negation is the only answer to finding the ultimate truth - it is as simple as that.

To see and feel nature from within means *not asking what the world is*. Classification is a human achievement which separates the human from nature—and separation always means conflict and unhappiness.

Continuous change and ultimate destruction after a certain duration is the very nature of all phenomena. Adversity and prosperity, happiness and misery, birth and death are inescapable aspects of the natural process of causality, but it is only anxiety and nothing else that is the root cause of suffering in this world. The man of wisdom, divorced from his senses, wants nothing, grieves for nothing, and fears nothing, and thus he lives in total freedom from anxiety.

Whoever is living this dream of life must necessarily continue in the dream until, through the grace of the *guru*, he is taken right out of the confines of space-time into the instantaneous apperception of his true nature. Only *then* will it be realized that what we call life is only a dream dreamt by THAT which we really are and that there never was in fact *anyone to realize anything*.

Any intelligent person will be convinced after only a little thought that security, as such, is a totally illusory concept in a world where the very *raison d'etre* is constant change.

Once there is a clear apprehension that an individual human being is an inseparable part of the totality of phenomenal manifestation and that he cannot pull himself out of the totality as an independent and autonomous entity, man naturally ceases to have personal intentions. When he is convinced that living is a sort of dreaming in which he cannot have any effective control either over his circumstances or his actions therein, all his tensions cease, and a sense of total freedom takes over. He then willingly and freely accepts whatever comes his way within the totality of functioning that this dream-life is.

The guru's instruction necessarily points towards Truth from within the ambit of conceptualization and time, but its *realization* by the disciple cannot be other than noumenal and therefore spontaneous, instantaneous and totally outside of conceptualization and time.

Life presents problems because we fight
life; we don't accept what-is in the present
moment. We want to become something
other than what we are. We want something other than what we now have.

Wanting to let go and the letting go are
two different things. The letting go will
happen only when you're not wanting to
let go.

Whatever has been happening, whatever
is happening and whatever will happen
can only happen according to His Will.

What is thought to be the 'unconscious'
mind is capable of a higher wisdom than
anything attainable by logic and reason.

Happiness and sorrow, right and wrong,
good and evil are all mere attributes of the
mind.

The final proof of Truth is that all
thought of it has disappeared. To seek it
is to lose it. Therefore, pure understanding is all—not the means but the
end.

Every moment he thinks and acts as an
individual entity locks man deeper in
the double-bind of self-consciousness
wherein the very thought of spontaneous living prevents it. And any positive
effort to control the mind or let go of
oneself always only strengthens the ego.
Mind cannot be used to control mind.

This present moment is the eternal moment. There is no eternity but NOW, before time ever was.

The identification of the split-mind with its own image has resulted in the paralysis of always trying to *imagine* itself in every contemplated action, rather than in the free and spontaneous expression of *pure action* which is man's natural function.

The state of the fasting mind or NO-MIND is by no means a condition of idiotic vacuity but precisely the opposite: a state of perfect, natural virtuosity, intelligence and spontaneous power.

True happiness cannot arise until the identification with the body-mind apparatus is demolished.

The state of freedom comes about when the split-mind gives up the impossible task of controlling itself and surrenders to the realization of the futility of perpetually *thinking and acting and thinking about the action* all at the same time.

Understanding is never a fixed value but a sort of free flow, a fluid process of nature itself that freely irrigates by merging thought and action.

There is only one state. When corrupted and *tainted* by self-identification, it is known as an individual. When merely *tinted* by the sense of presence, of animated consciousness, it is the impersonal witnessing. When it remains in its pristine purity, *untainted* and *untinted* in primal repose, it is the Absolute.

All that we can dialectically conclude is
that it is conceptually impossible to comprehend what we are because *mind cannot transcend itself.*

Movement in Consciousness, and nothing else, constitutes the mind and all its
experience of the phenomenal universe.
To *realize* this is the cessation of thought
and liberation from the bondage of ego as
mind and experience.

The fool and the wise man are not different. They are merely looking in different directions. While the fool is looking only at his mentations, the wise man looks at Nothing or Infinity.

Personal identity is nothing more than an identification between the mind and the image which it has about itself, an image which is really an abstract of memories of events in the past. Indeed, it is this censored and edited imaginary abstract that is considered to be an individual!

Only what is spontaneous can be correct because it is free of separation and thus of ego. In living truly and freely there is no thought and therefore no separation between self and other. And spontaneous, thought-free living can only come out of spontaneous Understanding.

Who is it who thinks he must do something and achieve something? Once it is understood that identity is an erroneous concept, that the body is merely an experience in consciousness (like any other phenomenon), and that there is no one to exercise any volition, where is the question of anyone *doing* anything? Our lives are in fact being lived *for* us rather than *by* us.

Pain cannot be escaped - yet even greater pain lies in the effort to get away from it. You will try to escape from pain or insecurity so long as the 'me' keeps itself separate from experience.

The desire to achieve (which is also the fear of failure) is what makes the mind lose its fluidity through the rigidity induced by inhibition. This then gets translated into faulty execution of all our actions and compounds our inner conflict and neurotic tension.

The apparent differences that constitute our world of separate existences are not intrinsic but only in the eyes of the beholder.

Life and living is a flow, and if we accept that flow and get into that flow, life can be tremendously simple.

When there is no other, there is no fear, and when there is no fear, there is freedom.

Understand that there really is no doer and continue to act in life *as if* you are the doer; then the appropriate attitude of compassion gets developed.

Every sentient being begins to die from the moment it is created. A simple glance at the phenomenal manifestation in the correct perspective is enough to bring home to us the utter unreality of the process of life and death, which then gets translated naturally into sweet surrender to *That Which Is*.

The meaning of life is that life has no meaning other than the living of it as a dream over which one has really no control.

The simple truth is that *all* events are predetermined *outside of time*.

The fundamental and unchangeable fact is that there is no human being who can perform *any* act on his own, any more than can a puppet on strings.

Spontaneity is the essence of all natural action. In natural action the focus of interest remains neither in the past nor in the future but in the present moment, the still point of the turning world.

✧ ✧ ✧ ✧ ✧

Once thinking as an individual has ceased, objectivization also ceases, and neither ignorance nor enlightenment has any significance. One who knows does not say, "I *think* I know." He Knows.

The question of enlightenment is generally viewed from the point of view of the individual. But whenever the phenomenon of enlightenment *does* occur, it is only by *other* individuals that a certain name and form is considered to have become enlightened. The individual concerned will have in fact *already disappeared* as an individual entity when enlightenment occurred.

All our feelings have significance only in relation to their relative opposites. Yet man, in his abysmal ignorance, forgets this basic fact of life and strives desperately for pleasure without pain and life without death! Without his realizing it, his viewpoint has become so distorted that he struggles after mere illusions, which leads to frustration and misery, finally culminating in the utter terror of physical death.

There is a center of attention, an awareness, that witnesses all opposites while
transcending them. This freedom from
good and evil, right and wrong, beauty
and ugliness is what is spoken of in the
Bible as the Kingdom of Heaven .

Since the human body is fundamentally
nothing but a swirling emptiness, a concentration of dancing energy patterns in
direct relationship with all other orga-
nized fields of rhythm throughout the entire universe, it is an obvious absurdity to
think that there can be any such thing as
a separate personal identity or an autonomous entity of any kind.

It is desire which is the only cause of bondage, irrespective of whether the desire is for some material benefit or for spiritual liberation.

The whole phenomenal manifestation is a product of the balanced interplay of tensions between polar opposites in a continuous integration and disintegration of changing forms in Consciousness.

It is the swallowing up of all differences
that brings into light and points the finger
at our impersonal source - the true nature
of what we ARE.

Self-realization is the result of going back,
reversing, reconsidering and finding out
what you were a hundred years ago, before you were born. It is the very absence
of presence or absence of space and time.

There is basically no difference between the waking state and that of dream, except that one *seems* more stable than the other. Only after there is awakening in the form of enlightenment is it realized that the waking world itself is indeed nothing but a long dream resulting from mental disposition - a movement in Consciousness in which what seems a solid body and its sufferings are really an illusion.

The nature of Consciousness is such that it simultaneously pervades the past, present and future and can experience infinite varieties of universes. But all is merely the play of Consciousness itself.

You just do not exist as an individual entity. Either you are nothing or everything, and either way the startling conclusion is inescapable—you are neither what you appear to be nor what you think you are but the Self whose phenomenal absence is the presence of all phenomenal appearance.

The very existence of the manifestation depends on its being perceived. Space and time do not otherwise exist. When the sense of presence as consciousness is not there, there *is* no manifestation. The only truth is BEINGNESS, here and now.

Truth conceptualized and vocalized is no longer Truth. Only where the perception has become entirely non-relational to objects has true awakening occurred. The essence of Truth cannot in any way be conceived but lies strictly in the *experiencing* of it.

The whole point of life is to live NOW in this present moment, always. If one makes a fetish of improving conditions in the future, one lives neither in the apparent present nor in the illusory future.

Seeking good to the exclusion of evil, or pleasure to the exclusion of pain, is like asking for there to be stars to the exclusion of space.

We can neither know nor become THAT which we already ARE.

It is a curious fact that one's chances of survival are best when there is no anxiety to survive. There is a special effectiveness or power of virtuality that is available to those who do not exhaust and dissipate themselves with anxiety. The subtlety, however, is that anxiety also *includes* any positive effort to *eliminate* anxiety—and this is precisely where true understanding comes into its own by accepting wholeheartedly whatever life brings without resistance or recoil.

✧   ✧   ✧   ✧   ✧

One can no more have an 'experience' of death than one can 'experience' deep sleep since there is *no one there* in either case to experience anything!

The intellect divides everything between what it considers pleasant (acceptable) and unpleasant (unacceptable) and then opposes anything it deems unacceptable as a "problem" that needs solving! Thus, any problem can only be solved at its source, which is the intellect that conceived the problem as a problem in the first place.

In comparison with the inconceivable Infinity that we actually are, what we think we are is a mere hallucination, an illusory and insubstantial shadow.

All phenomena are basically without existence. What is real is formless and invulnerable, while all that appears is subject to change and dissolution.

When in accord with the inevitable flow of causation, any apparent act of volition or free-will is merely an ineffectual and vain gesture, and when in disaccord with the inevitable resembles the frustrated fluttering of a caged bird. The fact is that there cannot be free-will *because there is no such thing as an individual entity* to exercise it!

In the case of the full apprehension of the
Truth, every perceptible thing, including
one's body, is realized to be nothing but a
product of the mind. Therefore, nothing
is seen to have any separate existence.
There is no self and no other but only the
impartial functioning of the total manifestation.

All experiences, from normal everyday
events to so-called 'death-experiences',
are only movements in consciousness and
therefore of the nature of dreaming. Experience can happen only to the ego, and it
just cannot be denied that the ego is
purely a concept, an illusion that has no
actual existence. Only when this false
identify of the ego is totally annihilated, is
there the realization of true BEING.

Bondage is nothing more than the illusion
that you are an autonomous entity.

Our identification with the subject-
versus-object convention is so powerful
that we cannot grasp the fact that there
can be knowing or understanding without a knower and a thing known. This
inability to put down the ghost of the
individual entity is the basis of our obsession with security and especially of our
great apprehension of "What will happen
to me when I die?"

For one who has become desireless, can there be anything to think or say or do? In his case everything happens *spontaneously, effortlessly and inevitably*.

Intellectual communication is useless because it is a temporal phenomenon with a triad of speaker, listener and what is said. It invariably concerns interpretation by the mind, which varies from moment to moment and from person to person. Intuitive communication, however, is immediate and without interpretation because it is Truth itself. The *intuitive* listener, the seeker with an open and receptive mind, will on some occasion feel an intuitive tug at the heart that may make him leap with the sheer joy that is ETERNITY.

All preconceived notions are insurmount-
able obstructions in the path of the arrow
of the *guru's* word toward the target of
the disciple's heart. The quickest, and per-
haps the *only*, way for enlightenment to
happen is for the disciple to listen to the
guru with a totally open, free and vacant
mind.

The one who has transcended conceptualization and thus sees nothing as other
than himself has nothing more to think
about or meditate upon.

The *perceiver* can never be perceived, and
what is perceived cannot be the perceiver.
It is only the ONE, cosmic awareness that
does the perceiving through all body-
mind organisms.

Understanding can come only at the appropriate time, and no one can say when.
All that *can* be said is that the understanding cannot come so long as there is
expectation, so long as there is a "me"
wanting it.

The phenomenal world is like a shadow which cannot exist without an object to cast it. It is dependent on something else for its existence. In this sense the phenomenal world is unreal, as it is a reflection of the noumenon.

We have no control over an arising of a thought or an arising of fear or anger or whatever. Arising of any thought, emotion or feeling is independent of the organism.

The guru makes no distinction between the great and small when offering the golden gift of salvation. He is always there as a guide to all, pointing to THAT which is the real nature of *all* seekers.

The individual self can exist only as a process of becoming, whereas THAT WHICH IS is the perennial state of BE-ING. Therefore, its realization is the annihilation of the individual.

Words can only *point* at Truth. It is only nonverbal, noumenal *understanding* that can deliver it.

By usurping the impersonal subjectivity of the one Absolute subject as that of an individual person, the human being commits the original sin and therefore comes under bondage. As soon as this mistaken identity is realized and the true identity as the one formless and eternal subject or witness is established, the bondage disappears and there is enlightenment.

The sage lives in a sense of equanimity so constant that he is impervious to pleasure or pain, gain or loss, praise or criticism. He is so vacant of volition that for him there is nothing to be done or not to be done.

True understanding comes about only after ignorance in the form of all conceptual knowledge is given up.

The very nature of the mind is to produce thoughts, and any kind of suppression of thought can only make matters worse. One need only *witness* all thoughts and desires as they arise and not get involved in them. Such witnessing in the end does away with one's identification as a separate bodily entity.

What man truly is neither suffers any experience nor exercises any such thing as free will. Neither is it subject to any such thing as destiny.

Anyone who has truly apprehended that it is impossible for him to live independently according to his own "will power" would naturally *cease having any intentions*. When he is convinced that living is a sort of dreaming in which he has no control over his actions, *all tension ceases and a sense of total freedom takes over*.

Whatever is perceivable is perishable, but your true nature is that which is neither perceivable nor perishable.

Living (existence) is a spatial illusion,
while dying (non-existence) is a temporal
illusion. When the light of consciousness
gets shut off, we no longer exist because
we are no longer elaborated in space and
extended in duration. But as what we
ARE we have never lived and we cannot
die.

Because it has been man's conditioning
that it is only effort which could bring him
anything in life, it is extremely difficult for
an ordinary man to grasp the fact that
nothing more than a deep understanding
of one's true nature is necessary for the
total transformation of awakening to take
place.

The illusory individual, along with the rest of the phenomenal manifestation, disappears into its Source as soon as its involvement in the process of conceptualization ceases.

Man's conflict and unhappiness stem from his obsessive preoccupation with security and survival based on two fundamental misconceptions: one, that he is separate and distinct from the rest of creation, and two, that he has independent free will in the choice of action to determine the results of events within that creation. This tremendous misunderstanding itself constitutes man's fall from divine grace, referred to in the Biblical fable of Adam and Eve as 'the knowledge of good and evil'.

Man's great illusion of happiness and suffering will never stop except by the mind's learning to *cease to act upon itself*.

Once you see the false as false, there is no further necessity to seek Truth.

The peculiarly subtle element in spontaneous, free or natural action is that it cannot result from effort of any kind, either positively by taking thought or negatively by *not* taking thought.

When you understand that actions which take place through your own body-mind organism are not your actions and thus the actions which take place through other body-mind organisms are not their actions (whichever way they may seem to affect you), then there is deep understanding that what exists in all organisms, that which brings about *all* actions, is the same Consciousness.

The human being is merely an instrument created for an event to happen, and enlightenment is an event which happens as part of the functioning of Totality.

Some seek a million dollars, and some seek salvation. So if you had the choice (which you don't), I would suggest that you seek a million dollars because if you get a million dollars, there will be someone to enjoy those million dollars. But when enlightenment happens, there will be no "one" to enjoy anything.

The *jnani* or liberated sage no longer has an individual identity to be concerned or embarrassed about, and his psychosomatic apparatus, the body, carries out its normal functions in the normal way without his even being aware of them. The wisdom he speaks is being said not by an individual personality but by the universal Consciousness, which has no shape or form.

All effort is due to the illusory desire on the part of an illusory individual to attain an illusory goal. Effort is necessarily the condition of a mind turned outward into conceptualization. When the mind turns inward into itself, conceptualizing ceases naturally and there is nothing left to make effort about or anyone left to do it.

Any action taken to suppress desire can
only strengthen it. Desire can only fall
away gradually by itself.

It is a rather curious fact that each man
craves for certainty and security as an
intrinsic part of happiness for himself, but
*without any clear idea of what this 'him-
self' is*!

Phenomenal manifestation has not taken place *separately* for human beings to perceive and cognize it but merely *includes* human beings. Its perception by them is necessarily false because in such perception both the supposed subject and object are nothing but appearances in Consciousness.

Conceptualization being the barrier to self-realization, almost every spiritual teacher has emphasized the necessity of killing the mind. Nonetheless, it is that very mind or intellect that has to be used to come to that point where it may be annihilated in Self-realization.

While we think it is we ourselves who are making the decisions, events are actually happening on a vastly magnificent scale in which we are merely pawns on a chess-board. Free will has, in fact, no bearing at all.

When you find out your source, the seed of your beingness, you will know the seed of the entire universe.

You dream that you are awake, you dream that you are asleep - and you do not realize you are dreaming because you are still in the dream! Indeed, when you *do* realize that this is all a dream, you will have *already awakened*.

One who has seen his true nature no longer regards life as being full of menace and misery as most people do. His previously mistaken sense of personal volition and responsibility has disappeared in such freedom and joy that life is now just an amusing spectacle like a game or a dream, in which he has no real part.

Enlightenment is the *inevitable* result of
the utter absence of purposeful intention.

Once submerged in the ocean of bliss and
knowledge, one cannot remain separate
from anything or *as* anything.

Logic and interpretation are limited to the framework of the relative intellect and cannot reach the level of the intuitive potential of the non relative Absolute.

We are already the noumenal Absolute, and we do not need any relative knowledge for the apprehension of WHAT IS. Knowledge is as much of a burden as ignorance. When both are thrown away, our natural Knowingness shines in its original pristine brilliance.

The sense of duality which is a barrier to
true love must prevail so long as the apperception of Truth has not occurred.
Once individuality is surrendered, there
is only total LOVE.

The covering of delusion and suffering
that has come over our original state of
unicity is nothing other than volition or
desire - the wanting of something to be
other than it *is*. All that is necessary is to
realize the falsehood of the ego and, by
inference, the falseness of all its demands.

An ordinary person *undergoes* experience, while the Self-realized one *Is* the experience itself.

The transcendental understanding of which the sages speak cannot be transferred or transmitted. It must *happen* in the effortless silence of the phenomenal void, and there is no way to *get* it through exertion or effort.

The counter question to every problem is:
"*Who* has this problem?" The realization
that he who has the problem is merely a
concept without any substance is the only
solution.

Everything happens altogether by itself.
The shadow of causation can never be
caught because all things and events are
merely interconnected differentiations in
form of a single, unified field.

Belief, any belief, is based on the sense of
insecurity. Only when all belief is given
up are you free to know yourself. In self-
discovery what you find is the Truth - that
Truth which is total, self-evident and
which needs no outside support or justi-
fication.

Fabricating objects in the split-mind is
what is called "thinking." But thinking is
not man's real nature - it is what *prevents*
us from seeing our real nature. Yet there
cannot be any prescriptive method to
bring about the cessation of thinking because any such effort would emanate
from a "me" that is itself nothing but a
product of thought.

Modern life is a vicious circle in almost every respect. The individual has reached a point where he actually thinks that it is *he* with his intellect who makes the world run. Yet, his very will, based on memory, is the product of a brain totally disassociated from the wisdom of nature that in fact operates it!

Whatever is happening is always happening only in the mind that perceives it.

There is only one state of being. There is not a single moment when one is not conscious of being. What we are in our sentient state is the consciousness of being present. When this conscious awareness is aware of sensory forms, it operates as witnessing. When it identifies itself with a witnessing organism as a separate entity, it operates as an individual person who suffers and enjoys.

The very idea of seeking one's true nature, the very idea of wanting enlightenment, is itself the biggest obstruction.

If changes are necessary, they will happen. And if something changes, you do something new or you cease doing something, there's no need to feel any guilt. It's part of the functioning of Totality.

When a person finds that his own efforts are fruitless, then he turns to a power, he *creates* a power, conceives a power, which will give him what he himself cannot get. He creates a concept, worships it, prays to it and begs it to give him what he wants. When even that entity fails to give him what he is seeking, further frustration and misery arise.

That man of understanding who has lost his identity as a separate individual remains identified with pure, infinite Consciousness while he continues to live out his life as an ordinary person in the world, knowing full well, however, that it is *all* an illusion.

Words, being merely the product of temporal conceptualization, have only the most limited usefulness. They can point to or describe a mango, but they can neither yield its flavor nor alleviate anyone's hunger.

No personal, individual effort can possibly lead to enlightenment. On the contrary, what is necessary is to rest helpless in beingness, knowing that we are nothing—to be in the nothingness of the no-mind state in which all conceptualizing has subsided into passive witnessing. In this state whatever happens will be not our doing but the pure universal functioning to which we have relinquished all control.

It is nothing but the personalization of the impersonal Consciousness as individual identity that constitutes the infamous 'ignorance' from which liberation is sought. And liberation, or true knowledge, is the realization that this identity is merely an illusion, a temporary aberration, like the shadow of a passing cloud.

By knowing for an absolute fact that he does not live but is *being lived*, the man of wisdom is aware of the perfect futility of all intentions.

For a nonentity there is no anxiety or worry, only a sense of incredible, total freedom.

Rare in the world is one who no longer even cares for experience. In him the true understanding has already dawned.

He who has gone beyond mentation has no need for sitting in meditation. His mind is already free from fluctuation.

The sage lives in complete apprehension of the fact that there is no individual doing anything, whether it be writing, walking, talking or anything else. Thus, he may be said to walk a thousand miles without setting a foot outside of his house or speak for forty years without saying a word.

The human being as an entity is only the result of thought, of the accumulated and constantly repeating conditioning that there is *something* in us which survives through time. Thus our private identity has been established in each of us as our own personal tradition.

Thought, desire and fear are all based on
time or duration through memory - they
are not of the present moment. They disappear along with time itself when volition has been abandoned or surrendered.

Man frees himself from the world, its ills,
its suffering, its chaos simply by seeing
the absurdity of it all.

It is only the body-mind apparatus that is involved in, or reacts to, any experience, and it can react only according to the way it is genetically made and shaped by past conditioning. Therefore, what is there to worry about or try to change? The one who understands Truth knows for a fact, "I do nothing at all."

The manifest is but the changing appearance of That which remains forever unchanged.

Consciousness is all there is. Seeing one thing, *you see it all*.

Let seeing see outward, and all it will see is objects. Let seeing see inward, and it will see not objects but that which is seeing.

No volitional factor can interfere with the operation of the process of causation. The very manifestation and its functioning is a non-volitional affair - indeed a dream in which the individual human being is merely an appearance, a puppet. To live non-volitionally is to cease to objectify and interpret on the basis of name and form. It is to live in absolute freedom.

Whether its aim is sensual pleasure, wealth or even enlightenment, desire remains desire. But when desire itself has been eliminated through the understanding of its endless futility, the outward flow of the mind disappears and the mind becomes vacant, perceiving the phenomenal universe as the mere *appearance* in Consciousness that it is.

The only way that worry will stop is through the proper understanding that change is the very basis of life, that we cannot continuously have something we like. We've got to be prepared to accept things in life which may not be acceptable.

When there is true understanding, there is an unqualified, joyous acceptance of the fact that life and living is not a stagnant pool but running water which cannot be stored in a bucket.

The basic point to understand and accept is that, whatever you do, the consequences are not in your hands.

Even the wrong-doing which results in suffering is part of the functioning of Totality, part of God's will.

"This too shall pass." Accepting this will bring about a double-sided effect. When something is bad, you will know this too will change, so there's no need to go into the depths of despair. When something is good, you won't have to go into the peaks of ecstasy. This too will pass. You will be able to accept life as it comes.

Things are actually without substance. Both things and the individual experiencing them are the same process, and not perceiving this fact is *also* part of the same process. There is nothing to be done about it, and there is nothing not to be done about it. What IS is *all there is*.

There is no causal relationship between
Consciousness and the universe. The
truth is that Consciousness alone exists
and is immanent in what *appears* as the
universe. They are not *two*, by which any
sort of relationship could exist.

You might prepare yourself to accept the
thesis that everything in the universe is an
illusion, yet you will more than likely fail
to include in this illusion the most essential factor, which is *yourself*.

Apperception of the highest Truth is not, and cannot be, a matter of gradual practice. Apperception, in fact, occurs prior to consciousness, which is the basis of intellect. It can only happen by itself, spontaneously and instantaneously. It is not in time, and there are no stages in which deliberate progress is made. Furthermore, there is NO ONE to make any progress.

The *implicit* meaning in any question is, "What about ME?" — but there never *was* a 'me' and never *can* be a 'me'.

What must happen will inevitably happen, without exception. There is no kind of intensity of supposed volition of any supposed individual that can in the least alter the inexorable causation of the Totality. *No one can will anything but what the Totality causes him to will*!

We are neither different nor separate from Consciousness, and for that very reason we cannot 'apprehend' it. Nor can we 'integrate' with it because we have never been *other* than it. Consciousness can *never* be understood in relative terms. Therefore, there is nothing to be 'done' about it. All is Consciousness and we are That.

It is impossible to describe the sense of
magnificence that comes out of the true
apperception of the nature of the individual in relation to the manifestation. The
loss of personal individuality is ex-
changed for the gain of the Totality of the
cosmos.

That which is beyond all interrelated opposites and relativity itself is Absolute
and inexpressible in words.

Although thought, words, logic and reasoning are obviously necessary to lead a moral life, they do not by themselves constitute *living*. They are all based on memory of the known and are products of the split-mind, the mind divided by the intrusion of a spurious 'me'. To LIVE without thought, without words, is to be receptive to the *unknown* with the *whole mind*.

True teaching is in reality the SILENCE of the SILENCE in which there is neither talking nor the absence of talking. It is like drawing the figure of a fish on the water's surface with a stick.

The sage is one who has offered as a sacrifice his own individuality, and this annihilation of identity is tantamount to a merging with the Totality in complete love.

What you *appear* to be is the outer body perceiving the outer world, but what you *are* is that Consciousness in which the body and the world appear.

The very first step in understanding is in giving up the false concept of 'I' as a separate entity. It is also the last step.

The existence of ego is purely conceptual. When a person sleeps, consciousness is absent, but he is not dead. We are neither the warm body that is alive nor the cold body that is dead. We are the birthless and deathless vital current of Consciousness itself.

Man's continuous attempt to freeze time in fixed moments out of the purposeless swirling of its dance is the cause of his frustration, fear and insecurity.

People are so absorbed in chasing what they consider to be happiness that they do not have either the time or the inclination to stop and wonder if the kind of happiness they imagine is even worth having.

Like the weak fibers that acquire great
strength when braided into a rope, illusion repeated innumerable times in memory acquires the strength of reality.

In REALITY, nothing is actually done.

All concepts arise from the Self and, if not
pursued, will subside back into the Self.

You will find it almost impossible to dis-
sociate yourself from your name and form
as an entity. This can only happen when
that which *thinks of itself* has itself disappeared.

It must be deeply and intuitively perceived that the seeker IS the sought. When this happens, the seeker himself has vanished.

The nature of mind is such that whatever we experience is actually nothing other than what we are.

Spontaneous, natural action happens only when the mind is vacant of the slightest trace of intention or planning. The greatest liberty is in having *total trust* in that final authority that makes the grass grow and our limbs, organs and minds work by themselves.

❖   ❖   ❖   ❖   ❖

The final understanding cannot be *achieved*. It can only be *accepted* when it arises as spontaneously and suddenly as a strike of lightning.

All human problems arise only because the basic fact of phenomenal manifestation is ignored - that the entire manifestation is *merely conceptual*. Nothing is created, nothing is destroyed. All questions pertaining to birth, life, death or rebirth are therefore utterly misconceived. WHAT IS is truly simple. We only make it complicated and incomprehensible by thinking and philosophizing about it.

✧   ✧   ✧   ✧   ✧

Feelings and emotions are all based on duality. So long as they continue to dominate one's outlook, duality will continue to have a firm hold, excluding the real holiness, the wholeness that is UNICITY.

What constitutes bondage or hindrance to Realization is *not* activity or even effort but *the sense of personal doership*.

Both ignorance and enlightenment are states of the mind, and the mind is not an *entity* but a mere *notion* inferred by the memory of experience.

The knowledge you are seeking about your true state is *unknowable* because comprehension at the mind level is only conceptual and therefore totally illusory. What you are seeking is what you AL-READY ARE.

We neither exist nor not exist. Our true nature is neither presence nor absence but the annihilation of both.

Even the very idea of the wholeness of the Absolute can only be a concept in consciousness. When consciousness merges in the Absolute, who or what can there be left to know or experience anything?

Desire to capture Reality at the mind-level means trying to confine the unknown and unknowable within the parameters of the known—it cannot be done!

Realizing one's true nature requires no phenomenal efforts. Enlightenment cannot be attained or forced; it can only *happen*. So long as there is a pseudo-entity considering itself a seeker working toward enlightenment, for just so long will enlightenment be prevented from happening.

Personal identity and enlightenment cannot go together. Indeed, there is actually no such thing as either personal identity or enlightenment, and the apperception of this fact is itself enlightenment.

All that we can truly say is, 'I am *here* in the absence of space and *now* in the absence of time', and the one thing that matters is the instantaneous apperception of this fact.

The truest advice for anyone listening to the teaching of Truth is to *apperceive directly and forget immediately*.

All effort at controlling thoughts, appetites and desires cannot but strengthen them along with the ego. Whatever has to go must fall off by itself. All that you are concerned with, all that you are, is the impersonal functioning of understanding. So let that understanding work through witnessing without judgement, knowing that there is nothing else that you *can* do.

Meditation and all such methods and efforts are distractions from simply abiding in the natural state which is one's limitless, real being.

All that is necessary for enlightenment to occur is the clear understanding that it is an utterly different dimension from mere intellectual comprehension, the dimension of BEING, to which no rigorous discipline or set practices can even be relevant.

Seekers continue to practice all kinds of self-torture without realizing that such 'spiritual practice' is a reinforcement of the very ego that prevents them from their natural, free state.

True understanding, which is enlightenment, can happen only when there is total effortlessness - in other words, in the utter *absence of any comprehender*. Then there is only the witnessing of the dream of life without the least desire to change anything.

Whatever action happens, whether you eat ice cream or meditate, at that moment you could not have done otherwise.

The ultimate realization is not only that the world is unreal but that at the same time the world *is* real!

In this drama of life, Consciousness plays and directs all of the roles of the billions of human beings. Every character is played by Consciousness.

The problem of how to live *does not exist* for one who is firmly established in the understanding of the nature of Reality.

The *guru* is not someone outside our-selves, he is immanent within us. He speaks directly as impersonal Consciousness, and therefore his teaching will only be available according to one's capacity to imbibe it.

Life is merely a series of movements in Consciousness, events to which we needlessly give a sense of volition as our own actions. So long as there is a belief that we ourselves are doing something as a factual entity, the necessary condition basic to awakening cannot arise.

Our error lies not in nature but in our attitude which demands that the course of nature halt at some particular moment of our well-being.

What we truly ARE is the everlasting,
unchanging moment which merely witnesses the play of changing relationships
that we call life.

How can you find true happiness? For
happiness, no positive action is necessary
or even possible. Turn yourself inward as
the pure, impersonal witness, and you
will rest in your true BEINGNESS in utter
peace and tranquility. Happiness will become irrelevant.

To accept that insecurity is an intrinsic
part of what we call life, and to *become*
that understanding, is to take a qualitative
jump from the relativity of involvement
to the non-relativity of pure witnessing.

Your life is only a series of automatically
conditioned reflexes very far removed
from the deliberate and purposeful action
of free-will that you suppose it to be.

The reality and permanence of the object that one imagines oneself to be is an illusory continuity like that of a river, which *appears* to remain the same yet is composed of entirely different water from one moment to the next.

The question of what will happen to me when I die is indeed as misconceived as the question of what happens to my lap when I stand up or to my fist when I open my hand.

Until there is the conviction in the seeker that all phenomena, including himself, are merely appearances without any substance, there can be no true understanding.

You are the primordial state of total freedom, that fullness of pure joy, that concentration of light which is subtler than the subtlest and the witness of everything.

When the mind is let alone to be one with space so that the mental space becomes united with the physical space, then all that remains inside and outside is 'I' Consciousness, the fullness of pure BEING.

The origin of all psychological misery is the basic separation assumed between self and non-self. We are so habituated to accept separation and boundaries as a natural phenomenon that it is an enormous surprise to be shown the world as it truly is.

You cannot catch your own shadow, and
neither can you escape it. So long as man
thinks in terms of phenomena being real,
the shadow of ignorance will both evade
and haunt him.

Just as waves arising on the surface of
water have no independent existence and
are only the water itself, so also are manifested phenomena only the apparent created form or body of the Unmanifest.

Insofar as you keep watching the mind and discover yourself as its witness, nothing else can project itself on the screen of consciousness. This is so because two things cannot occupy the attention at the same moment. Therefore, delve within, and find out where thoughts arise. Seek the source of all thought, and acquire the Self-knowledge which is the awakening of Truth.

The way to the realization of Truth is neither through attachment nor renunciation. There is in fact *no way*. No means of any kind can either indicate or grasp the Ultimate.

TRUTH is the most obvious thing one could find, or not find, and any intricacies in the understanding of it are, without doubt, entirely of our own making through our incorrigible habit of conceptualizing everything. If one but stops conceptualizing, TRUTH is staring us in the face!

We can truly experience only what we ARE as 'I'. There is absolutely nothing else to be experienced, or that *can* be experienced. There is no need to make any effort to recover that which we have never lost.

The root of all trouble, that which prevents the seeing of Truth, is desire. Desire in *any* form is the only obstacle, *even if that desire is for liberation*!

The Self neither comes nor goes. For that Consciousness in which the universe appears and disappears there is neither gain nor loss.

Other than Consciousness nothing exists. Whatever you see is your own reflection. It is only through ignorance of your true nature that the universe appears to exist. One who understands with conviction that the universe is nothing but an illusion becomes free of it.

Thought works only on memory, and man's likes and dislikes are based on previous experiences. Without the mediacy of thought, neither likes nor dislikes arise, nor is there any attachment to experience.

To seek enlightenment as an individual identified with a body is to continue to suffer misery. Unless you forget *everything*, you will never be established in the Self.

Although one may be afraid of the process of dying, deep down one very definitely has the feeling, the intuitive conviction, that one cannot cease to exist. This feeling has been misrepresented as the basis for the theory of rebirth, but the fact of the matter is that *there exists no actual entity* to be either born or reborn or to cease to exist.

The absence of intentions (because there is no one to have them) is true understanding. When no individual exists, what remains is enlightenment.

Unabidance in the ego is abidance in the Self.

The sooner the identification with the body as a separate entity is lost, the sooner will the grace of the guru blossom in the consciousness of the disciple.

In Truth there is neither any path nor anyone to go anywhere on it. There is nothing to attain, nothing to achieve, because without knowing it you are *already* Home.

What characterizes the rare one, the wise one, is the fact that he lives in this world as if he is not in it. He is in fact not even concerned whether he lives or dies. He thinks and lives vertically in a world that moves horizontally. Hence, he remains unintelligible and unrecognizable to the average person.

Thinking about the Unthinkable is still only another aspect of thought. To see the illusory nature of the universe is primarily to see the illusory nature of *oneself*.

Though in itself limited, a developed intellect is nonetheless necessary as the one faculty that can bring us to the brink of true Advaitic understanding. The person with a keen intellect becomes enlightened even when the instruction of the guru is imparted casually, whereas without it the immature seeker continues to remain confused even after a lifetime of seeking.

A mature and penetrating intellect will not have divorced itself from intuition and bound itself so extensively in logic and reason as to obstruct its natural receptivity to the spontaneous arising of divinity.

In enlightenment basically, whether it happens through understanding or through devotional surrender or whether it happens through good deeds being done in such a way that there is no "me" doing them, there is just one common thing. The common factor is that there is no sense of personal doership. There is no "me."

You are the reality, you cannot talk of reality. The moment you talk or think of something, it is in phenomenality and therefore conceptual.

There is neither up nor down nor inside
nor outside nor without nor within. All
there is is Consciousness. And this manifestation is an appearance within that
Consciousness. And even that appearance is only an objective expression of the
same Consciousness. All there is is Consciousness.

You are merely an instrument through
which Consciousness is functioning.

In the eternal moment, the present moment, there is no "me" and there is no duration—no past, present and future. And when there is no "me" and no sense of duration, all there is is that silence in which conceptualization cannot take place.

Self-abidance cannot be acquired. It is something which arises spontaneously when the mind is free of the concept of acquiring.

The nature of the mind-intellect is to project itself outward towards the acquisition of knowledge about the universe and its functioning. But knowledge can only be of what is itself illusory and unreal. The pursuit of such knowledge merely prolongs ignorance through continuation of the false identity of the knower. Unless this process is reversed and the enquiry has turned inward, the discovery of man's true nature and the true nature of the universe cannot even begin.

❖　❖　❖　❖　❖

All phenomena are the objective expression of the subjective 'I'. Before, during, and after the illusion of existence, there is only one REALITY.

We cannot apprehend Consciousness because we have never been other than it. We cannot integrate with Consciousness because we are never disintegrated from it. In relative terms we can *never* understand what Consciousness is. The Whole-Mind cannot be known by the split-mind of relativity.

Enlightenment being THAT which is prior to experience, the expectation on the part of the seeker to 'experience' enlightenment is not unlike the blind man who wants to understand the nature of the world around him while insisting that it must only exist in the same darkness to which he is subject.

It is futile to seek human reason, purpose or meaning in the events of life, which are in fact impersonal and not human at all.

The intuitive apprehension that is real faith is based on a certain inescapable inevitability, a relaxed acceptance of WHAT IS that is totally free of any doubt or opinion.

To live in the eternity of the perpetual present is to be in perfect accord with *immanent natural law*, in which there is neither right nor wrong.

Contentment can only dwell in the heart of one who is happy with *whatever* befalls him in life.

Whatever happens in the working of the universe at the present moment has to be accepted. Not accepting it means human misery.

If some Power has turned you into a seeker, don't you think it is the responsibility of that Power to take you where you are supposed to be taken?

The billions of human organisms are merely instruments through which God or Totality or Consciousness is functioning. It is the only power that has been functioning all these thousands of years, and it is that power that is functioning now and that power that will continue to function. It is an illusion for us to think that we are doing whatever we are doing.

You cannot chase God. At the right time and place God will chase you.

The Self-realized sage responds TO-TALLY to whatever prevails in every moment - without the least intervention of the mind.

That the human being is not, and *cannot* be, an autonomous and self-willed entity is made obvious by the fact that in the absence of consciousness there is no sentience, no intellect and no manifest world - and over the presence or absence of consciousness no one has any control whatsoever.

The entire manifestation is purely conceptual. Nothing has actually ever been created, and nothing has ever been destroyed.

Words can never transfer understanding. They can only open the way for one's intuition to rise into consciousness.

Enlightenment means nothing more than to be rid of conceptual thinking. What remains is the noumenal 'I', pure subjectivity without the slightest touch of objectivity or temporality. But instead of simply being this, we mistakenly try to get it as an object of experience.

You cannot possibly *own* anything because you *are* everything.

The illusion of 'future' is created by the divided or split-mind as its own imagined projection, whereas the natural whole-mind knows no future because it lives totally in the present REALITY, which is eternity itself.

Man is so enslaved by the conditioning of conventionality that most of the time it smothers all spontaneity. What is necessary is not surrender to the mad urges of caprice but the profoundest recognition of that intelligence with which man is already naturally endowed.

In seeing with the whole-mind, intuitively, the apparent seer disappears and the seeing becomes the seen.

Any kind of seeking presupposes something that is sought which is different from, or other than, the one who is seeking it just as whatever is found presupposes the one who has found it. Indeed, the one who thinks he is enlightened is as much in bondage as another who thinks he is ignorant.

Seeking *must* continue until final frustration results in the surrender and disappearance of the seeker himself.

The inherent weakness in any form of meditation is that it necessarily implies activity and effort based on the existence of a separate entity who will make this effort, while the very object of meditation is the final disappearance of any such entity. Not by any amount of effort can one elude one's own shadow!

No rational explanation is possible in regard to the universe or the ways of providence. The divided mind, which operates only in duality, is incapable of knowing or understanding the WHOLE, that undivided universal Consciousness which is its own source and the source of everything else.

The essence of manifest existence is continuous change, from integration or birth to disintegration or death. With sentience comes the will to live, to not yield to disintegration, and this is the ego, which generates the thinking mind and all man's misery in the ensuing futile attempt to avoid the inevitable.

True love of God means surrender to Him, wanting nothing- *not even salvation*.

A mind that can apprehend an object *as it truly is* will know precisely nothing at all. Such is the whole-mind of the enlightened sage.

When the personal consciousness realizes
its universality, it sees the great dream of
creation for what it is—an enormous joke!

When the heart suddenly opens itself to
the supreme Truth and is filled with the
bliss of the Absolute, then this very world
is realized as an abode of bliss.

The wise man makes efforts *without con-cern for their results* because he is aware that he has no choice regarding either. True awareness leads to spontaneous and unerring action *without the intervention of the mind*.

Real happiness can exist only when con-ceptualization has ceased.

The actions of the liberated one are free like the movement of wind. Having transcended worldly existence, he lives in the world as if without a body. Therefore, he is without concern and has nothing to gain or lose anywhere.

Any thought or notion that arises in the mind is provoked by an outside stimulus for which the corresponding image or substance is evoked from memory. This is how thought is born. Thus, the reality of any object, whether as near as a chair or as far as a star, stands only as an image in the mind. And mind being nothing but the content of consciousness, where there is no consciousness there is neither mind nor universe.

The arising of a thought, emotion or desire is something beyond the control of the organism. The nature of the mind can be either to "take delivery of" and get involved in it or, when the "me" is not there, the arising of it is witnessed and it disappears.

The naturally virtuous man goes about his business, and the things which happen through him are virtuous because there is no personal intention. There is nothing personal he wants from anybody.

The virtue and unpretentious naturalness
of the sage often goes unnoticed because
of its ordinariness.

The sage, or the wise man, is well aware
of the artificialities of the world of men.

The word "accident" means something happening without premeditation, without cause. And yet we always ask who caused an accident. The mind always wants to know who is responsible.

The wise one has become free merely by *understanding* what freedom is. The fool tries to attain it through personal effort and must inevitably fail. When the fool finally *gives up*, then he himself becomes wise and free.

The arising of an experience, an event, is totally outside the control of any body-mind organism whether enlightenment has happened or not.

A body-mind organism in which enlightenment has happened doesn't become a vegetable. Thoughts will arise. Emotions arise. But those thoughts or emotions or desires are not taken delivery of. They just happen.

If an event is accepted and it is accepted that the instrument through which the event occurred is not of the essence, it is so much simpler to be transformed from personality to Impersonality, from individualism to the Universality.

Tranquility means acceptance of what is without wanting to change it. Acceptance of what oneself is without wanting to become something else is freedom.

The mind, being nothing more than the stream of thoughts, obviously cannot be extinguished by either the desire or the decision to do so, which itself is a mere thought. The mind, which is the ego, is only fattened by such exertions.

The ostensible purpose of all meditation is the cessation of thinking or conceptualization, but this can never be achieved by any entity because an entity is itself the thinking process. A deep understanding of this truth, however, can itself lead to a spontaneous fasting of the mind, whereby thought ceases effortlessly on its own, as would a clock cease whose winding has been allowed to run down.

Awakening cannot take place so long as
the idea persists that one is a seeker. Doing *sadhana* means assuming the existence of a phantom. The entity that you
think you are is false. You ARE the Reality!

It is fallacious to think that there is an
individual self which functions through
the body and the mind. The 'me' as an
individual self is merely a mental modifi-
cation, and there is no such thing as a
mind apart from thought. When the source
of thought is probed continuously as it
arises, it is revealed that there is no such
thing as mind or an individual behind it.

The hazard of any kind of disciplinary practice or meditation is that the means and the end generally get utterly confused. Some seekers end up in frustration when they find that long years of such practice have brought them nothing, whereas others may go along the Pathless Path and reach the Destination Which Is No Destination almost effortlessly, while yet others fall by the wayside having mistaken some puerile spiritual power as the ultimate goal. The subtle and fundamental fact that is most often missed is that the means and the end are one and the same, and that the only means to Truth is Truth itself — *Understanding is all.*

The truth is that all *search* for Truth must end in failure. The one must awaken who was never asleep, and the one must sleep who was never awake.

That mind which ceases to *grasp at itself* achieves its original pristine purity and becomes *unborn* and whole again.

The man who has freed himself through understanding accepts whatever comes his way without any judgement and remains within the underlying unity that encompasses man and nature in the totality that is the universe. He wanders through the enjoyment of all experience without becoming attached in any way, either positively to delights or negatively against sorrows, and thus remains free in all circumstances.

No one is born, no one dies. What is born is only a concept. There is no entity to be freed. Not understanding this fact is the bondage of ignorance. Apperception of it is the freedom of truth. And the apperception of truth is not in time - it is always instantaneous.

You might see the whole universe as a dream, but so long as there is still a *you* (a separate entity) seeing this dream, you will continue to remain confused.

The unfortunate result of all efforts at self-improvement is that the ego creates further and deeper separation *within* itself, defeating its own purpose by strengthening the very source of separation and conflict that the ego itself *is*. Such efforts lead at best to mental frustration and at worst to total insanity.

You can neither effect nor avoid change because change is life itself, just as the flow *is* the river. To attempt to resist or provoke change is futile, and there is no other way but to *realize* it. The inexorable flow of causation is not to be influenced by a mere shadow of its own expression, which is all that a human being is.

Who is the perceiver? Universal Consciousness alone is the perceiver. The body is merely the mechanism through which perceiving takes place and from which the ego is *inferred* as the perceiver of other objects. Strictly speaking, there is neither the perceiver nor the perceived. There is only perceiv*ing* as the objective expression of the subjective functioning of the one Universal Consciousness.

The notion of individual volition has been referred to as "the bite of the deadly serpent of ego" because it is the very root of the concept of bondage or unhappiness, and the *only* thing which can free man from its poison is the abandonment of his identification with a particular object as a 'me'.

The ordinary, ignorant person can only see things as objects seen by a subject. Then, with a certain shift of understanding away from separate personal identity, it dawns on him that only the impersonal subject is real while the objects themselves are illusory. Finally, with total enlightenment, the sage sees objects as objects once again but within an essential unity where there is no separation of subject from object, or in fact any separation of any kind.

The *guru's* grace is always there for all to carry away in ample measure, but there is no rule as to when or where it will fructify. All that the *guru* does, and all the he *can* do, is to point to THAT which we all are, and if there are no obstructions like doubts or intellectual vanity or inordinate attachment to things material, the transformation can be immediate. In fact, it *has* to be immediate. Otherwise it will be nothing more than intellectual knowledge.

The only proof of absolute Truth is not in *knowing* it, because it cannot be known, but in BEING IT.

An apperception of the basic meaninglessness of conventional values, in terms of reality, lifts man out of the apparent strife and conflict of life. He now sees life as a game in which he must participate according to the rules but which he need not take at all seriously.

Spontaneous action will take place irrespective of conceptual volition or intention. In fact, strictly speaking, *all* action is spontaneous action. It is for this reason that a man of true understanding is usually an enigma to most people—precisely because his actions are natural and spontaneous, they are completely unpredictable!

It is when the mind gets involved that a problem becomes a problem. Otherwise it is just a thought. And if that thought is merely witnessed, it disappears.

The basic understanding has to be that no
"me" is special. The human being is
merely part of the totality of manifestation.

As acceptance gradually expands, then
life becomes easier. Suffering becomes
more easily bearable than when you are
looking at it as something to be rejected,
something to be ended.

Personal volition drops off naturally for him who has come to the deep conviction that as an apparent individual he does not live as an entity but is merely *being lived* by the dream-structure of this manifestation.

To think in terms of doing something or refraining from doing something with the intention that a subsequent event may or may not occur is a view based on the misconception that the future depends on our volitional actions of today. It is this false premise of autonomy that sustains the utter futility of what we consider our volitional actions and their consequences of retribution or reward. There is, in fact, neither volition nor cause and effect but only an indivisible Totality of Functioning that appears as the manifest universe.

Insecurity can never disappear until the sense of separation itself disappears.

There is *actually* only seeing—neither the seer nor the object seen exists apart from the *process* that seeing is.

Real understanding does not solve problems, it *dissolves* them.

The presence of a 'me' in any activity, including spiritual practice, insures the continuance of desire and the perpetuation of fruitless effort.

Breathing goes on by itself while the de-
luded individual thinks it is *he* who is
breathing. Thoughts come from outside,
arising spontaneously through intervals
of mental vacuum, and he thinks it is *he*
who is thinking. The thoughts get transformed involuntarily into action, and he
thinks it is *he* who is acting. All the while,
he is doing nothing but to misconstrue the
actions of the Totality as his own action.

❖   ❖   ❖   ❖   ❖

Just as the flow of a river ceases once it
reaches the sea, so also do all disciplines
and effort for liberation cease when one
meets the *guru*. Meanwhile, what is the
use of accepting the illusory nature of the
universe and everything in it while excluding yourself?

From the standpoint of Truth there never was any fruit to be obtained by making spiritual efforts, there is nothing to be acquired, and whatever IS has always been there.

Self-enquiry is essentially an investigation into the true nature of man because, whatever he may think of the world outside and whatever he may conceive of as God the creator, it is conjecture and conceptualization based on the only thing of which he can be certain, the only thing he actually *knows*: that he exists, that he is *present*, that he lives by the feeling of BEING.

The root of frustration which the civilized man feels today lies in the fact that he lives not in the present moment but for the illusory future, the future which is only a creation of brain and therefore a mere inference based on memory, a futile abstraction at best.

It is impossible in life to have the pleasure that is wanted without the pain that is not wanted. They are in fact mutually interdependent and therefore inseparable.

The central point of the ultimate understanding is that at any and every instant
there is nothing but perfection in the totality of functioning that is the universe.
Thus, the present moment and whatever
it offers is accepted in total and uninhib-
ited pure enjoyment.

Volition and responsibility are unnecessarily assumed by the individual for acts
and events that are *all* really subject to
determination by what is called causation
or destiny.

What may appear to be changes in the nature or character of an individual from experiences of divine love, universal brotherhood, or physical or psychic ecstasy are nonetheless *affective phenomena* and therefore movements in consciousness, not Self-realization.

Life is truly great—if you don't get *involved* in it.

Pain and pleasure exist for animals, but it is not a problem for them because the animal does not regret the past pain or fear the future danger. He lives in the NOW of nature. It is only the human being who concerns himself with *imagined opposites* as a problem. There are, in fact, no opposites whatsoever except as concepts produced by the imagination.

The pure Consciousness that is infinite and eternal is forever free from all modifications.

You and I are not two but the same Absolute Unicity.

❖   ❖   ❖   ❖   ❖

The *guru* is always there and ready with grace. All that is needed on the part of the disciple is the capacity, the requisite kind of receptivity, to accept it. Nature does the rest.

True worship is effortless, supreme meditation in the continuous, unbroken awareness of the within, the indwelling presence. It requires no effort because there is nothing in it to be attained which one does not already possess.

What is generally understood to be prayer is nothing more than one fictitious entity called 'me' begging for something from another fictitious entity called 'God'.

The broad perspective, the floodlight which is the perfect understanding, sees things as they are.

Security means no change, and nothing in the universe can remain unchanged. The human being's search for security must necessarily end in frustration. The human being has to accept that insecurity, the changing from one opposite into the other, is the very basis of life and existence.

Seeking starts with the individual and
ends with the total annihilation of the
individual.

Freedom is what happens when the arro-
gant and silly notion that we live our own
lives by our own will has fallen off.

The thinker himself cannot possibly effect the cessation of thought. Insofar as he is involved in the thought of ceasing to think, he himself *is* the perpetuation of thought. But if the thought process is merely watched or impartially witnessed, it will subside on its own and take the thinker with it.

Spiritual practices are based on the false identification of the seeker with the ego and its efforts, attributing to the Self various defects and limitations *conceived by the ego*. But the manifestation of the universe is itself an illusion in which the same ego is included only as a helpless and finite part. So *who* is to make any effort, and for *what*? That Self which is sought through Self-enquiry is already realized because there is nothing *but* the Self.

All the "me's" and "you's" are merely the objective expression of the one subjective "I." The sudden realization of this often reduces the individual to a state of explosive, uncontrollable laughter at the primeval joke that is this whole illusion of creation.

Our natural state, as an intrinsic part of the Totality, is one of utter relaxation. It is only the separation from this Totality (through our illusion of free-will) that brings out fear, aggression and the tension of insecurity. And it is only through surrender to this Totality that all such unnatural tensions are eliminated from our system.

The spontaneous abandonment of purposeful intention is the only way by which enlightenment can happen. Without intention there is no will, no 'me' and no egocentric effort, but only the natural, noumenal ACTION of living.

From the viewpoint of the illusory individual entity, problems will never cease. From the viewpoint of the totality of phenomenal functioning, problems never arise. Deep understanding of this is itself the master key which will open the door to the peace that is joy, the joy that is FREEDOM.

Spiritual awakening carries no remnants.
The awakened live deeply established in
the apperception that they and the universe are merely appearances.

'I' was the same 'I' fifty years ago or five
hundred years ago or even before time
ever was, and 'I' shall be the same fifty
years hence or five hundred years hence
or even after time ceases to be. While time
passes by, 'I' am forever unchanged.

If you would disidentify from the body
and remain firmly entrenched in that animating Consciousness which gives you
sentience and the sense of presence, I AM,
you will know peace and total freedom in
this very moment.

The self-realized sage is not perfect, he is
TOTAL.

Silence is the most powerful medium for transmission of this knowledge — for this knowledge to arrive intuitively.

The basis of spirituality is not guilt or burden. The basis of spirituality is relaxed freedom.

Emotion, like a thought or a desire, arises in the mind. The arising of any thought or emotion or desire is always spontaneous. You cannot *will* a particular emotion to arise nor can you keep it from arising.

When mind is vacant, it is free. When conceptualization has ceased, there is no one to be concerned with anything. When the mind remains aloof from sensory functions, which in themselves are merely the working of nature, there is no suffering but only the freedom of natural action. Where there is no more notion of personal doership or non-doership, all action becomes non-action.

Real understanding translates itself into spontaneous and uncontrived activity through the same latent power of virtuality that exhibits itself in the miraculous fruition of plants, the formation of eyes and ears, the circulation of blood and the subtle reticulation of nerves. Such power is generated without conscious direction, and the man who has it will usually be so steeped in ordinariness and anonymity as to go unnoticed by others. Yet his action will be the purest, most effective and powerful of all action precisely because it coincides with the universal process itself, without any sense of volition whatsoever.

Wisdom is inherent in the total acceptance of every situation as it is, with the awareness of witnessing everything as though in a dream, keeping trust in the basic and essential harmony that is the unpreconceived natural intelligence of the universe.

Actionless activity succeeds by *being* rather than doing, by *attitude* rather than act, by *compassion* rather than compulsion, by *humanity and tolerance* rather than force and aggression.

While the nature of sleep, trance, fainting and death may differ somewhat, in each case the surrender of consciousness and individual identity is essentially the same and accompanied by a loss of awareness, while enlightenment is the surrender of consciousness and individual identity in a state of total Awareness.

Self-enquiry is a passive rather than an active process. Mind is *allowed* to subside into its source even while engaged in normal activity, which then becomes an undercurrent of witnessing that gradually extends throughout all waking hours and begins to pervade all one's activities without intruding on them or interfering with them.

If you remain as you are now, you are in the wakeful state. This is abolished in the dream state. The dream state disappears when you are in deep sleep. The three states come and go, but *you* are always there. Your *real* state, that of Consciousness itself, continues to exist always and forever, and it is the only Reality.

Tranquility comes only in the utter absence of resistance to the experience of the present moment and therefore has nothing to do with idealistic intellectual commitments to either action or non-action or to any other conceivable aspect of idealized behavior.

It is intellectual conceptualization that raises various unnecessary issues, gets the individual trapped in its net, and makes him forget the fundamental question as to *who* and *what* the questioner himself really is.

You cannot ask that love be created in you. You cannot turn toward God until the turning away from the self has occurred.

Every experience is an impersonal experience. The personal experience loses its impersonality when the mind-intellect accepts this experience as its very own, accepts it or rejects it as good or bad.

Seeking begins with the individual and
ends when the individual seeker realizes
that all this time what he has been seeking
is what he actually *is*, that the seeker *is* the
sought, that there never had been an individual seeking.

Thoughts are bound to arise. The trick is
not to get *involved* but to simply ignore
them altogether.

It is only resistance that transforms the
eternity of the present moment into the
transience of passing experience as time
or duration. Without resistance there is
only *eternity*.

Real virtue cannot be cultivated. It can
only be the inevitable, natural consequence of understanding itself.

God is merely one of man's concepts, a
symbol used for pointing the way to the
Ultimate Reality which has been mistaken
for the Reality itself. The *map* has been
mistaken for the actual *territory*.

Worshipers may derive some sort of satisfaction or peace of mind through worship of a concept such as God (created by
themselves), but it is a futile process from
the viewpoint of experiencing one's true
nature.

Genuine joy, which has no counterpart in sorrow, has no reason whatsoever. All reasons belong to phenomenal relativity, whereas pure joy is of the entirely different dimension of causeless noumenality.

All deliberate effort to improve anything in life cannot but end up in self-contradiction. Absolutely no effort is necessary to live life fully. It is like floating with the current or rolling with the punch—while the sturdy oak gets pulled down by the storm, the pliant grass remains supple and swaying.

Every attempt at controlling our inherent nature results only in suppression and its adverse consequences. All that one can do is live according to the inherent nature of one's psychosomatic apparatus and let the understanding of our true nature deepen and work such changes as are necessary without any thinking or volition on our part.

Whatever change is needed, *happens*. Whatever happens *must* happen. All that one need "do" is to *cease having doubts*. This is true *faith*.

Only when it is *time* in the cosmic scheme of evolution for a particular psychosomatic apparatus to get enlightened can enlightenment *happen*. And if that time has come, nothing in this world can prevent it from happening. Nor can anything in this world *make* enlightenment happen if it is *not* time.

Once one has *known* the self-generating spontaneity of the happening of all events, an absence of seeming volition or control is no longer a frightening matter but a joyous celebration of freedom.

Until the conviction arises that the entire universe is just a dream, it is futile to try to give up anything, and such conviction cannot begin to arise until such time as sensory enjoyment has been sufficiently experienced for one to have realized its essential hollowness.

True understanding is of the same nature as the simple knowledge I AM - that I am alive, that I exist, and that I do not need anyone else's confirmation to prove that I am alive and present.

He whose sense of personal doership has dropped off through intuitive in-seeing of his nature finds no reason to speak or do anything. Though in the eyes of ordinary people he may seem to lead a normal working life, for him *nothing exists*.

Solitude is never a function of place, but of mind. A man attached to desires cannot get solitude anywhere, whereas a detached man is always in solitude wherever he may be.

Whatever may be taking place at any particular time, the question of right or wrong, correct or incorrect, improving or not, is truly irrelevant. You cannot help doing precisely what you are doing.

If what you have heard here appeals to your heart, only then accept it.

You may think you are doing something. I *assure* you, you are not. There is no individual doer.

The malignity of all problems arises precisely where there is a mistaken identification with a body-mind apparatus as a separate entity that *thinks it is in control of itself.*

When Realization dawns, then what happens? You are no longer 'you'. You remain established in the inner silence and freedom without any concern for your welfare, content with whatever comes along - and life goes on in perfect effortlessness.

When you see that you have no control over the results, you stop worrying about the results and concentrate on the work that is being done.

If we accept life from day to day, from moment to moment, we'll find that life can be amazingly simple.

If you've heard something here, fine. If not, fine. If some change is to occur as a consequence, let it take place. If the understanding at any level has any value, any worth, it must work its own way out.

The universe is uncaused, like a net of jewels in which each is but a reflection of all the others in a fantastic interrelated harmony without end.